CW00348872

The
Golden
Game Fair

The
Golden
Game Fair

Written & Compiled by
Chris Newton and Tony Jackson

ELLESMERE
The Medlar Press
2008

Published by the Medlar Press Limited,
The Grange, Ellesmere, Shropshire.
www.medlarpress.com

ISBN 978-1-899600-82-3

The CLA Game Fair and the Publishers would like
to thank all those who have contributed photographs, anecdotes and
their memories of the Game Fair to make this book possible.

The CLA Game Fair and the Publishers have made every attempt to contact
copyright holders but if any have been inadvertently overlooked
they will be pleased to make the necessary arrangements.

Produced in England by the Medlar Press Limited, Ellesmere.
Designed and typeset in 11 on 13pt Baskerville Roman by
Jonathan Ward-Allen.

Contents

Foreword

By HRH The Duke of Edinburgh

Over the last 150 years the British countryside has been subject to a major social and agricultural revolution. There was a time when the populations living in the great urban-industrial areas were roughly balanced by those who inhabited the country towns and villages. Not only has the total population grown, but the rural population has shrunk. It is, therefore, hardly surprising that the majority, who live in and around our great cities have lost touch with the realities and traditions of country life.

The first to notice this trend, not surprisingly, were the farmers, as their livelihoods depended on it. They responded by turning their agricultural shows into 'shop-windows' for townsfolk to see where their food was coming from. However, the production of food is not the only activity that takes place in the countryside. The most important of these activities, is the daily, monthly, yearly and century continuation of the life of our planet, as we see it in our island. Agriculture makes use of this process, but agriculture is not the sole exploiter of the natural system. It should not be surprising that people who live in the countryside have used the natural system to provide them with sports and entertainment. Our hills, forests and rivers, and the game which inhabits them, are still available to those who have to work in cities.

50 years ago the Country Land and Business Association had the courage and foresight to support, what turned out to be, a brilliant idea to stage a Game Fair. The intention was to encourage people from all walks of life to understand how the countryside works, and to have the opportunity to see at first hand the many pleasures that it can offer. This book is the record of how that first Game Fair was created, how it grew and prospered, and, particularly, how it is achieving its purpose.

Introduction

Celebrating 50 years of the CLA Game Fair

It is 52 years since two men from the ICI Game Research Station put their heads together and came up with a new kind of social event to bring together the shooting and landowning interests of the British countryside. On the Saturday of this year's Game Fair - July 26 2008 - it will be 50 years to the day since their idea became reality in the form of the first Game Fair.

The idea would have been stillborn had it not been for the enterprising decision by the Board of the Country Land and Business Association (then the Country Landowners' Association) to throw their support behind the event. It is a decision the Association has never regretted.

In half a century the CLA Game Fair has grown and widened its appeal far beyond the expectations of the men who founded it. And yet through all the political, commercial and social changes that have buffeted the countryside and those who live and work there over the past five decades, the Fair remains in 2008 essentially what it was in 1958 - an opportunity for country people of varying interests and backgrounds to get together to chew the fat, exchange skills, wisdom and experience, and do business together.

Today the CLA Game Fair stands proud as the leading event in the countryside calendar. We are proud to present this history of the Fair's eventful first 50 years.

1

In the Beginning

1956-7

Today, The Game Fair without the Country Land and Business Association would be like Old Trafford without Manchester United. But it could all have been so different.

Back in 1956, a small group of men from the Game Research Station (eventually to become the Wildlife & Game Conservation Trust, via the Game Conservancy) had the idea of bringing the British shooting community together for a weekend. They started by asking the British Fields Sports Society for sponsorship. It would be a perfect forum, they pointed out, to promote the sport of shooting, and a tremendous recruitment opportunity for the Society.

The chaps from the BFSS weren't so sure. They thought about the idea for a long time, but in the end they turned it down. Instead, the GRS men turned to the CLA - then the Country Landowners' Association - and ushered in a piece of history.

The first seed was sown at Crufts. In the years after World War II, the second day of that famous show would focus on gundogs. The day made a natural meeting point for gamekeepers and provided a valuable opportunity for them to exchange news and ideas and discover how other shoots and estates were faring. Many a landowner would give his keeper a fiver and send him off to enjoy himself for the day with his friends and peers.

The focal point for these encounters was the ICI Game Research Station stand. Its staff would dispense advice on practical game management, while keepers from up and down the country would meet to discuss everything from the treatment of gapeworm to hedgerow management, game crops and poult feed (this was still the era of warm mashes containing boiled rabbit, eggs and a variety of secret potions devised by keepers from older generations).

Enjoyable and valuable as these occasions were, the Game Research Station men recognised a need for something more; a proper forum for the exchange of knowledge among the shooting world, to satisfy the great interest among keepers in emerging scientifically-based ideas about game management.

The result was a decision to put on special courses for keepers at the Game Research Station's HQ, Burgate Manor, near Fordingbridge in Hampshire. As only 60 people could be catered for at any one time, the GRS men soon began extending the courses to three or four days. To make them more convenient and more widely accessible, they also decided to make them into a 'moveable feast' by staging them at a variety of venues around the country.

Against the background of the booming post-war interest in game shooting, the courses caught on more quickly than the organisers had expected. There was clearly room to take them further - much further.

In July 1956, Nigel Gray, senior game advisor at the Game Research Station, had an inspired idea. Why not create a national event at which keepers and landowners could get together to discuss ideas, explore aspects of the sport and, at the same time, help to promote it?

He put the idea to his friend and colleague Charles Coles, Deputy Director of the GRS and later to become Director of the Game Conservancy. Coles was enthusiastic, and suggested they go further by turning the event into a small-scale public show, featuring clay shooting and gundog trials. He had been involved in falconry, and felt that this little-recognised sport would be a useful addition to the bill. The two men calculated that it ought to be possible to offer sufficient demonstrations, competitions and exhibitions to provide the basis for an interesting day - perhaps two.

Dog handlers, clay shooters, falconers, game farmers and shoot owners were consulted for their reaction to the idea. They indicated a cautious consensus that it might work, at least on a limited scale. There was just enough enthusiasm to persuade Gray and Coles to test the water by putting on a trial event for the summer of 1958.

The first problem was to find a suitable site. East Anglia appeared the obvious choice, containing as it did a large shooting population and offering reasonable access to London and the Midlands. Gray located an abandoned wartime airfield with a number

Nigel Gray (left) and Charles Coles

of Nissen huts which he thought could be converted into lecture rooms, trade stands and refreshment rooms. They decided to invite agricultural and forestry specialists and perhaps a few game farmers, gundog enthusiasts and clay pigeon shooters to contribute.

The ad hoc 'committee' thought that initially the event might attract 500 people, and they would need parking for 200 cars. With a bit of luck and a following wind, they thought they might just double that figure.

But the airfield idea soon got the bullet. A much better proposition came up: Hall Farm, a shooting estate at Stetchworth, three miles to the west of Newmarket in Suffolk and the property of the Earl of Ellesmere. Hall Farm had the lot: a magnificent range of buildings, extensive fields, handsome belts of beech trees and, best of all, a welcoming and enthusiastic agent, Major Raymond Elkerton. Lord Ellesmere, the absentee landlord - he was living in Scotland - promised the venture his unqualified blessing, on the condition that he would not have to get involved himself. The keepers and estate

13

staff needed no convincing about the new venture and embraced the project readily.

'They were magnificent buildings, laid out almost as if intentionally for a show' wrote Nigel Gray in a later Game Fair programme article about the founding days. 'Fine big fields and handsome beech belts - it all added up to as near perfect a site as we could wish.'

There now remained the small matter of finding some exhibitors. Gray and Coles decided to approach potential supporters individually to announce their new venture and explain how it could benefit those who took part. They drew up a target list of possible companies and organisations, headed by the gunmakers, game farmers and fishing tackle manufacturers, and split it between them, Gray taking on the tackle manufacturers as he was an angler himself. Then, in between doing their regular daytime jobs at the Game Research Station, they set to work contacting their prospects to explain the new venture and to ask for their support.

At first, it was heavy going. The firms had no experience of selling their wares at an open-air event of this kind, and their reaction was sceptical.

Fortunately, there were some notable exceptions. Holland & Holland, Gaybird Pheasant Farm - then one of the largest game farms in the country - and *The Field* magazine gave their assent and support immediately. Reassured by the presence of such prominent names on the participants' list, others began to follow their lead. The stage had been found, and the cast list was filling up nicely.

There remained a crucial issue to be tackled. Gray and Coles had to find a sponsor - a national body with the authority, the public image, the experience and the resources to front the whole event and take responsibility for its success or failure. The obvious choice was the British Field Sports Society, the parent body of game shooting. Charles Coles knew its Secretary, Brigadier Pepys, so he made an appointment to meet him at his London office.

'The organisation was then very stuffy and old-fashioned and was really much more interested in hunting than the other field sports. Nevertheless, I thought it was a great opportunity for them' he says. 'I explained what we were planning to do and outlined the benefits to the Society.'

The BFSS, he assured Pepys, would profit from massive publicity and, as a result, would be sure to recruit hundreds of new members. Nothing could be more appropriate than the Society's association with a major new national event for the rural game shooting community. It could simultaneously raise the profile of the society and change the future of game shooting.

'Pepys told us we would have to wait for the idea to be put to the board. His main concern was who was going to pay for it, and he wanted to know if ICI would pick up the tab in the event that we lost money. That was out of the question of course, as we had to have an impartial, non-commercial sponsor; we needed the BFSS to underwrite it. We explained that the benefits to the society would far outweigh any small loss that might be made on the gate.

'Once he heard ICI would not foot the bill, Pepys told us we could forget the idea. It really was a great missed opportunity.'

That left just one option. Coles and Gray knew that the only other organisation with the resources to take on the new event was the Country Landowners' Association. Coles arranged a meeting with John Ruggles-Brise (later Sir John), its President, and Francis Taylor, Director General.

This was a time when Britain's landowners had been on the defensive for years. The emphasis at the Ministry of Agriculture was firmly on commodities and production grants, and crop prices were fixed annually. Not everyone agreed with this approach, but the National Farmers' Union had great power, and wielded considerable influence at MAFF.

With wartime hardship and post-war rationing still fresh in the public mind, food production was king. Hedges were scrubbed up, wetlands drained, watercourses dredged and canalised. According to Charles Clover in his recent series on the history of the CLA for *Country Landowner*, 'Millions of acres of moorland and permanent pasture that had not been ploughed up during the war were "improved" by farmers with grants from the Ministry, sometimes to the rueful regret of their landlords.' It was not until the end of the 1970s - by which time 95 per cent of Britain's herb-rich meadows had been destroyed, along with many thousands of acres of relict woodland - that a more enlightened attitude would start to prevail.

Country sports were not, at this time, the most pressing issue on the CLA's agenda, and the link between the Association and the plan to hold a national country sports event might have appeared somewhat tenuous. Nevertheless, Sir John Ruggles-Brise responded eagerly to Coles and Gray's proposal. He could see the opportunities such an event would offer to both the CLA and the wider shooting world. After hearing his guests out, he declaimed: 'I think it's a winner!'

He wisely put one man in charge of organisation - Major Gee, a retired Gurkha officer. Gee was given the responsibility for all the practical arrangements - laying out the ground, booking stands and accommodation, marquee hire and insurance.

In July 1957, the CLA Council formally agreed with Ruggles-Brise's recommendation that the Association should sponsor the first Game Fair. Lord de Ramsey accepted the post of chairman of the Organising Committee, and Raymond Elkerton boldly and efficiently took on the job of organising secretary. The show was on the road.

This was a brave and imaginative decision on the part of the CLA. Today we accept country and sporting fairs as a routine part of the countryside calendar; back then, they were distinctly new-fangled. Very few people on the commercial side of the shooting world had any understanding of public shows and how to take part in them.

Costing the exercise was largely a matter of guesswork. Elkerton thought a budget of £500 would be sufficient to cover the cost of the Fair, and the committee accepted that figure.

Country Landowner, the CLA's bi-monthly magazine, confined its advance publicity of the event to a single cautious entry in its 'Headquarters Notes'. 'This is the first Fair of this kind to be held in the country, and it is hoped to attract sportsmen from a wide area of East Anglia and the Midlands' said the report, which went on to outline some of the planned exhibits.

The date was agreed as July 25 and 26 1958. With barely a year to go, the work of planning and preparation begin in earnest.

2

Uncharted Waters

1958: the first Game Fair

Charles Coles, Nigel Gray and the newly-elected Organising Committee had plenty of work to do in the months leading up to the first Game Fair. Buildings had to be repaired or converted; ground levelled and prepared for vehicles; supplies laid on for participants and visitors; catering and toilet facilities arranged; signposting planned and constructed.

Publicity was low-key by comparison with what was to follow, and was largely confined to a few discreet announcements in the sporting press.

The *Shooting Times* for the week before the Fair reminds us that not everything changes in game shooting. 'There can be few countries which regard their field sports as of so little national importance' wrote 'Tower Bird' (the Editor, Tim Sedgwick). 'Unsubsidised and unsupported by grants, denied even a proportion of the taxes spent in their name by those who take part in them, hunting, shooting and fishing depend almost entirely on voluntary subscription and effort for their existence. . . individually, the sportsman has always been notoriously apathetic about the machinations of the anti-sport fraternity. That his present state is no worse is due entirely to those associations that keep a watchful eye on his interests.'

As the weeks ticked away towards the due date, the weather obstinately refused to play ball. The summer of 1958 was a 'brute',

as Nigel Gray put it, and July was dominated by heavy rainfall. With the show due to start on Friday 25th, the little band of organisers despaired that it would ever stop. It was far too late to change their plans; all they could do was hope and pray.

But by the third week of July, with the Fair just a few days away, it was still raining. The CLA team was resigned to a soaking, and in all probability a humiliating flop.

At last, on the eve of the big day, the rain stopped and the clouds parted. Hopes began to pick up; perhaps they were not facing a disaster after all. 'We stood at the entrance like first-term schoolboys, scrubbed, brushed and with our hearts thumping inside our best suits' wrote Gray later.

But as the long-forgotten sun began to break through, it seemed the reprieve had come too late. The gates opened at 10am to a bare trickle of visitors. There were no waiting queues, no eager crowds of locals clutching their admission money, no cavalcades of vehicles bumping up the lane to the car park.

However, as the morning wore on and the sun strengthened, the waiting world seemed to get the message. The trickle became a flood. Within the hour the official numbers had already topped the 500 which the committee had thought realistic for the entire weekend. By noon, the crowd had passed the 1000 mark. Things were looking up.

Derek Cousins from Essex remembers it well; he was the second visitor to arrive in the car park on that first morning. 'A brilliant occasion' he calls it, thanks to the exceptionally friendly atmosphere. 'Though it wasn't as commercial as later Game Fairs were to become, there were still enough exhibitors to make it thoroughly interesting. I even bought a Webley 700 shotgun, at a ridiculously modest price.'

The entrance charges were equally modest; two shillings and six-pence per person admission (half price to children, free to CLA members), 5/6 ($27^1/_2$p) for cars and 2/6 ($12^1/_2$p) for motor cycles, while bicycles were free. For those without their own transport, the Eastern Counties Omnibus Company had laid on buses from Newmarket. A simply-produced, black-and-white 32-page programme with a two-colour cover was on sale at two shillings.

LIST OF FIRMS PARTICIPATING IN THE GAME FAIR

BLOCK A.

Buffet.
Messrs. Roffe,
41 Burleigh Street, Cambridge.

BLOCK B.

Forestry Commission.
G. F. Ballance, Esq.,
Divisional Officer,
The Forestry Commission,
(Eastern Conservancy), Block D,
Government Office,
Brooklands Avenue, Cambridge.

BLOCK C.

Gunmakers' Row.

1. James Purdey & Sons Ltd.,
   57 South Audley Street, London, W.1.
2. Cogswell & Harrison Ltd.,
   168 Piccadilly, London, W.1.
3. Westley Richards & Co., Ltd.,
   23 Conduit Street, London, W.1.
4. Rowland Wards, Piccadilly,
   London, W.1.
5. Holland & Holland Ltd.,
   98 New Bond Street, London, W.1.
6. Gallyon & Sons Ltd.,
   66 Bridge Street, Cambridge.
7. I. M. Crudgington Ltd.,
   7 Green Street, Bath.
8. Plant Protection Ltd., Publicity Dept.,
   Imperial Chemical House, Millbank,
   London, S.W.1.
9. I.C.I. Game Research Station,
   Fordingbridge, Hampshire.

BLOCK D.

Ministry of Agriculture.
The Regional Controller,
Brooklands Avenue, Cambridge.

BLOCK E.

1. St. Hubert's Club, St Hubert House,
   53 Green Street, London, W.1.
2. British Field Sports Society,
   51 Victoria Street, London, S.W.1.
3. Game Farmers' Association.
   Cotswold Game Farm Ltd.,
   Stroud, Gloucestershire.
4. Anglers' Co-operative Association,
   3 Dr. Johnson's Buildings,
   Temple, London, E.C.4.
5. The Wildfowlers' Association,
   19 Castle Street, Liverpool, 2.

BLOCK F.

1. The Animal Health Trust,
   14 Ashley Place S.W.1.
2. Mr. A. Wylie
   Rectory, Carlton, Newmarket.
3. Edward Webb & Sons
                (Stourbridge) Ltd.,
   Wordsley, Stourbridge, Worcestershire.
4. Mr. Richard Harrison, Harthover,
   Blackwater, Hampshire.
5. M. Dwight, Esq., The Pheasantries,
   Berkhamsted, Hertfordshire.
6. Dunns Farm Seeds Ltd.,
   Dunseed Chambers, Salisbury, Wilts.
7. Stephens Cabinet Incubator Co.,
   Hempstead Lane, Gloucester.
8. The Field, 8 Stratton Street,
   London W.1.

BLOCK G.

Gamekeepers' Club

1. Major A. W. Neve, Gamekeepers'
   Association. Mildenhall. Suffolk.

2. Messrs. Whitlock Bros.,
   Great Veldham, Essex.

BLOCK H.

1. Messrs. Christopher Hill, Ltd.,
   The Quay, Poole, Dorset.
2. The County Game Farm, Hothfield,
   Ashford, Kent.
3. Messrs. Keevil & Keevil Ltd.,
   Central Markets, London, E.C.1.
4. Messrs. Whitmores Timber Co.,
   Bury St. Edmunds, Suffolk.
5. Messrs. Edwards & Walkden, Ltd.,
   Central Markets, London, E.C.1.
6. Messrs. Girdlestone Refrigeration Ltd.,
   74a Burleigh Street, Cambridge.
7. Cotswold Gamefarm, Camp, Stroud,
   Gloucestershire

BLOCK J.

1. Messrs. D. McMaster (Bures) Ltd.,
   Mount Bures Works, Bures, Suffolk.

BLOCK K.

1. Warwickshire Pheasantries,
   Pailton, Nr. Rugby, Warwickshire

BLOCK L.

1. Messrs. Gilbertson & Page,
   Hertford, Hertfordshire.

BLOCK M.

1. Lincolnshire Pheasantries, Tumby,
   Mareham-le-Fen, Boston, Lincs.
2. Messrs. H. W. Hill, High Street,
   Newmarket, Suffolk.
3. E. G. Clarke & Son Ltd.,
   36 Station Road, Framlingham,
   Woodbridge, Suffolk.
4. Messrs. E. C. Longmate, Ltd.,
   Terrington St. John, Wisbech, Cambs.
5. Messrs. J. L. Newman & Sons,
   Hillside, Swaffham Bulbeck, Cambs.

BLOCK P.

1. S.A.P.P.A., Raingate Street,
   Bury St. Edmunds, Suffolk.
2. Eastern Electricity Board,
   High Street, Newmarket, Suffolk.
3. A. J. Ridley & Son Ltd.,
   40 Abbeygate Street,
   Bury St. Edmunds, Suffolk.
4. Messrs. Maywick Appliances Ltd.,
   Wickford, Essex.
5. A. S. Juniper & Co. Ltd.,
   5 Smithfield Markets, London, E.C.1.
6. Richardson & Preece,
   Witham, Essex.

NATIONAL PROVINCIAL BANK

LLOYDS BANK

G.P.O.

REARING FIELD.

1. Eastern Electricity Board.
2. Gaybird Pheasant Farm,
   Prestwood, Gt. Missenden, Bucks.
4. The Priory Waterfowl Farm.
5. The Cotswold Game Farm
6. County Game Farm,
   Home Farm, Hothfield, Ashford, Kent.
7. The Lincolnshire Pheasantries.
8. I.C.I.

In all there were 55 exhibitors, including gunmakers, game farm-ers, shooting and game rearing equipment suppliers, a brace of high street banks and a variety of public bodies and official organisations. The official programme featured 21 advertisers, including James Purdey, Cogswell & Harrison, Holland & Holland, Gilbertson & Page and the makers of the new four-wheel drive Austin Gipsy (Austin's short-lived response to the Land Rover, then just a decade old and revolutionising rural transport), while companies and asso-ciations who supplied prizes for competitions included *Shooting Times*, Gaybird Pheasant Farm, Henry Atkins Ltd, Gallyons, St Hubert's Club and Dwight's Pheasantries.

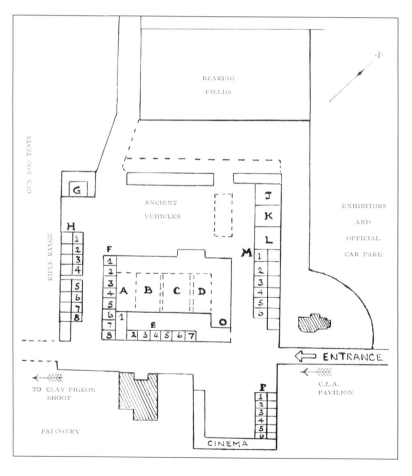

Gunmaker's Row was a rectangular block of nine stands rather than a row, but it was at the heart of the Fair, a position it has held ever since. As *The Field* put it: 'Gunmaker's Row dispelled, once and for always, the idea that guns must be sold from gloomy caverns of mahogany and glass'. In 1958 it featured just six gunmakers, plus the taxidermists Rowland Ward of Piccadilly, Plant Protection Ltd and the ICI Game Research Station. The Wildfowlers' Association (WAGBI) had a stand in a neighbouring block, as did the British Field Sports Society, the Anglers' Co-operative Association and the Forestry Commission, while there was a strong showing of game farms.

Cogswell and Harrison's eye-catching display featured a genuine cowboy pistol in a lavishly-tooled holster, which attracted great interest from the gamekeepers. Purdeys and Holland & Holland had craftsmen on their stands to demonstrate aspects of the gunmaker's art, while Westley Richards combined their stand with Rowland Ward to great effect. Rods from Farlow's were also on show.

Malcolm Lyell, then Managing Director of Westley Richards, remembers how amateurish it all seemed. 'We didn't know how to put together a proper stand. We were staying at my father's house near Newmarket, so we emptied two of his bookcases and transported them to the Fair to form the ends of the stand. Then we put up pictures, guns, rods and a couple of mounted heads for decoration. Guns were simply left lying on tables for people to look at. I don't think we sold very much, but that wasn't the point - it was the chance to meet up with others from the game-shooting world that mattered.'

The managing director of Boss, the famous gunmaker, had declined to take part - on the grounds that on the only occasion the firm had attended an exhibition, in Paris in 1910, they had failed to sell any guns.

The keepers had their own exclusive beer tent where they could meet and discuss the world of game rearing while their employers browsed the gleaming wares on display along Gunmaker's Row.

Charles Coles and Nigel Gray were there of course, doing their 'day jobs' by dispensing advice from the Game Research Station stand, and delighted at the success of their brainchild.

The British Field Sports Society had unbent sufficiently to agree to taking a stand at the Fair, and among the visitors on that first day was Coles and Gray's old friend Brigadier Pepys.

'He looked around in wonder at all the attractions and the crowds of happy people' says Coles. 'He told us "I didn't realise it was going to be like this!" I'm sure they regretted not having taken the chance to sponsor it.'

As for exhibitions and other attractions, visitors could watch a demonstration of peregrine flying by the British Falconers' Club, a display of vintage horse-drawn and mechanical vehicles used to carry game and Guns, a game rearing field showing the latest equipment, a clay pigeon shoot (organised by the Eastern Counties CPA), a small-bore rifle competition or an archery contest. They could also watch one of a series of films on sporting birds and game rearing topics.

The clay shooting event reminds us that this is not quite as new a sport as we might imagine. Concealed traps produced simulated going-away partridges, driven grouse and sprung teal.

Showground facilities included a mobile post office with a coin-operated phone box, a bank and a gamekeepers' club (organised by the Gamekeepers' Association). To get everyone in the mood, music was provided by the band of the 1st Battalion of the Cambridgeshire Regiment, TA.

There was a buffet and bar, and 'first class luncheons and teas' were available. Of public lavatories there is no mention; presumably it was not thought necessary to discuss such indelicate matters in print.

Celebrities were somewhat thin on the ground compared to today's Game Fairs, but there was certainly one; Bob Arnold, who played the gamekeeper Tom Forrest in *The Archers*, made an appearance on the Friday to sign photographs for fans. The production team recorded a scene at the Fair, which was included in that evening's episode.

This first Game Fair was very firmly focused on game shooting. Most of those who supported it, as exhibitors, sponsors or donors of prizes, were gunmakers, pheasant breeders or suppliers of pest control equipment; almost all were connected with the shooting sports in some way.

THE FIELD, *July 31 1958*

THANKS AND APPLAUSE for the Countess of Ellesmere after the prize-giving. On the left is Lord De Ramsey, and on the right is Sir John Ruggles-Brise.

PEOPLE AND SCENE

Pictures by LE

A pictorial account of both days' events on

THE RIFLE RANGE, for match and sporting ·22 rifles, where a trophy was given to the highest scorer with a match rifle on each day. Mr. B. R. Finch won on Friday, and Mr. M. Emery on Saturday.

A PANORAMA VIEW. The main "s

MR. ANDREW WYLIE, of the Pinehawk Gundog Kennels, with a litter of his English springer spaniels.

THREE VISITORS FROM NORFOLK: Mr. J. Stimpson, Brigadier Long, and Lord Walpole, the President of the Gamekeepers' Association.

LORD FAIR
In the backgr

THE FIELD, *July 31 1958*

THE GAME FAIR

'SON

llesmere's estate near Newmarket

MR. A. H. HAMILTON, from New Zealand (*centre*), talks to Mr. Douglas Middleton (*left*), manager of the I.C.I. Game Research Station at Fordingbridge, and his deputy, Mr. Charles Coles.

y morning before the day's crowds arrived.

THE CENTRE OF ATTRACTION wherever they went, these falconers are (*left to right*) Mr. Mavrogrodato, with his gyr falcon; Mr. P. Glazier, with a peregrine; Mrs. M. Woodford, with a merlin; and Mr. M. Woodford, with a goshawk. The falconry display was delayed several times because of unsuitable weather.

Quis and Marchioness of Cambridge of the Heaton Game Van, originally with Estate

SIR CHARLES BUNBURY, Bt. (*left*), the chairman of the East Suffolk branch of the C.I.A., talking with his son Mr. William Bunbury (*right*) and Major J. Holt-Wilson.

MR. R. W. ELKERTON, the chartered land agent who is agent for Lord Ellesmere, and who was the "Fair Secretary." The game cart behind him is the property of Lord Ellesmere.

Courtesy of The Field.

As the programme introduction explained: 'The aim of this first CLA Game Fair is to show how, with modern techniques of game rearing, a small shoot can be worked up without much trouble or expense . . . game can, in fact, be regarded as a useful supplementary crop and good sport helps to make up for some of the burdens and responsibilities of ownership'. One pictures the hard-working farmer taking a well-deserved day off to invite his pals over for a walk around the coverts with twelve-bores under their arms - a luxury not so many can afford today.

At this time game rearing was undergoing a transformation. Although most keepers were still using the movable pen in conjunction with broodies, we learn from the programme that 'the pen and broody system is now being superseded, to a certain extent, by new methods using artificial incubation and brooding with electricity, paraffin or calor gas for heating'. The rearing field exhibit at the Fair displayed the latest techniques developed and adopted by the Game Research Station.

The Game Fair plan shows that gundog tests were included, but there is no mention of them in the programme, nor of how they were organised or who took part. Angling did not feature.

Rifle shooting got a lengthy plug in the programme. The programme notes record that Britain then had 4500 rifle clubs, while the National Small-Bore Rifle Association had a membership of over 200,000.

The Forestry Commission set out its stall clearly in the programme. 'The staging of a Game Fair in Great Britain provides an opportunity for considering, in their proper relationship, the full economic opportunities of rural land use' it reminded us, going on to point out that planting woodlands would not only enhance shooting and contribute to revenue, but help the Commission in its target of establishing five million acres of well-managed woodlands over the next half century – coincidentally by 2008 (the figure was referring to planted coniferous woodland). The continuously-changing agenda for the countryside and its forestry over the intervening years makes it hard to see the wood for the trees when it comes to assessing whether this target has been achieved, but the Forestry Commission assures us that the trend has certainly been an upward one; the total amount of woodland cover has increased from 5% of the UK land area in 1924 to 12% today.

The rain returned on the Friday night, but the skies cleared again in the morning and the crowds returned. The final total attendance was reported as 8500 - seventeen times the committee's cautious original estimate.

The CLA was able to congratulate itself on a well-run event. Very little had gone wrong, with the exception of a somewhat over-subscribed catering service, at least on the first day. After totting up income and expenditure, Raymond Elkerton, who had performed such a splendid job as secretary, reported with embarrassment that the total cost for the first Game Fair had amounted to £800, a budget overrun of £300. The CLA committee were not too concerned; the prospects for the future looked bright indeed.

'What we saw, as anybody who was present will agree, was a genuine unrehearsed slice of English country life' wrote Wilson Stephens, Editor of *The Field*, the following year. 'The shooting men and their families, gamekeepers and their masters, were enjoying themselves in a manner which was as true a reflection of modern rural England as was the maypole of Merrie England centuries ago.'

The Field ran a four-page report on the Fair the following week. It called it a 'great occasion' and praised the CLA for transforming a bright idea into a resounding success. 'They have done a most notable thing - they have written a new occasion into Britain's sporting calendar' wrote the reporter, Peter Garnham.

'Just how much was achieved on July 25 and 26 1958 can hardly be calculated yet' he went on, concluding prophetically: 'In five years' time those dates will be seen to have made history by providing shooting men with a festival parallel to the Royal International Horse Show among horsemen.'

The event had 'the homely air of a garden party' despite its scale. 'Most memories will hold vivid pictures of old friends meeting under stately trees, of an encouraging turnout of keen young sons and grandsons and of a wealth of charming ladies.'

Shooting Times was equally full of praise for a 'first-class' show. 'The Game Fair must now be firmly established as an annual event for many years to come' wrote Tim Sedgwick in his leader. 'In spite of the crowds, at no time did one have the feeling common to most shows of oppressive overcrowding. This was due first to the layout of the stands and demonstrations, and secondly because there was so much to see that even those present on both days had to keep moving to cover the ground.

'Merlins and a peregrine flew to the lure where decorative archers in traditional Lincoln green had earlier given an exhibition of strength and fluent accuracy that made more than one expert rifle shot raise his hat. Muzzle-loader vied with breech-loader at high pheasants - and won. Labradors showed their paces - and more intelligence than allowed by the rules - in working tests; the modern simplicity of game rearing was ably explained, with all the props; for a shilling one could try to burst balloons, hit moving targets not much larger than clay pipes or attack the more leisurely five-bull card with a match rifle.

'To the music of the band of the Cambridgeshire Regiment keepers and landowners, tenants, farmers, rough shooters, fowlers, dog trainers, clay busters and countrymen from all points of the compass walked and talked and watched and learned and competed in friendly rivalry - no one criticised.'

The report in the August 1958 issue of *Country Landowner* made it clear that the Game Fair was here to stay.

'Everybody is saying - "This is a jolly good show - we must have it again: where is it going to be held next year?"' declared the report. 'In fact the CLA has decided to do it again elsewhere, and has booked the dates - further particulars to be announced later.'

The world did not have long to wait. Within weeks a venue had been chosen for the second Game Fair, and the work of planning and preparation was under way.

3

The Show Goes On

Into the 1960s

1959: Hackwood Park, Hampshire

The overwhelming success of the CLA's first Game Fair secured its place immediately as a permanent fixture in the sporting calendar. Within weeks of the 1958 event, the committee had agreed to hold another, on July 24-25 1959.

This time the venue would be Hackwood Park, near Basingstoke in Hampshire, by courtesy of the Rt Hon. the Viscount Camrose. Captain Robert Petre was asked to act as chairman, while Major Archie Coats, the renowned pigeon shooter, served as secretary, and Coats' wife Prue became in turn Coats' secretary.

The success of the first Fair had reached the ears of the Duke of Gloucester, who agreed to act as Patron and to attend - by helicopter - on the first day. He was to remain Patron until his death in 1974.

The idea of moving the Fair to a new venue each year was conceived early on, and it became a cornerstone of Game Fair philosophy. A fair which remained in one part of Britain could not

The Duke of Gloucester (left) and Captain R.C. (Bobby) Petre at Hackwood.

lay claim to being a national event. By turning it into a 'roadshow' which visited a different part of the country each year, the organisers could give as many people as possible the chance to visit this major national countryside event.

The Hackwood Game Fair was more confidently publicised than the maiden event had been; a car sticker was inserted in every copy of *Country Landowner* and readers exhorted to display it, and to urge their friends to come along. The souvenir programme (as it was described, for the first time) was more than twice the size of that printed for Stetchworth, running to 68 pages and packed with advertising. There were 91 exhibitors, some 60 per cent more than the previous year.

The crowds rolled in from the first moment, cheerfully paying the increased entrance fee of five shillings for access to such a big and promising event. Glorious weather throughout the weekend ensured that the event could not fail to be a huge hit with public and exhibitors alike. This 'Game Fair weather' came to be associated year after year with the Fair, with very few exceptions.

As before, CLA members could get in free on production of their membership cards. They could also enjoy the luxury of a members' 'luncheon marquee', with a fully-licensed 'lounge' and a cafeteria featuring an à la carte lunch with game pâté, smoked trout and salmon, and Game Fair pie. Unfortunately this offer proved a little too mouth-watering; *Country Landowner* reported that on the Friday 'hundreds' had converged upon the marquee simultaneously, leaving latecomers with nothing but crumbs.

An angling section had been considered for the first Game Fair, but there had not been quite enough support to make it happen in time for the Stetchworth event. By the following year, however, the angling world was promising support in plenty. Thus it was that in 1959 Fisherman's Row was born.

The first Fisherman's Row featured eleven assorted trade stands and casting competitions (entry 2/- for adults). These figures indicate that it had already overtaken Gunmaker's Row, with about the same number as the previous year, although Stephen Grant & Joseph Lang Ltd had joined.

Barrie Welham, one of the great names in the professional angling world, attended that Fair and went on to staff the Garcia stand at each one for the next 34 years. For many years he was one of the casting demonstrators, along with luminaries such as Captain Tommy Edwards of Hardy Bros, Col Esmond Drury and Pierre Creusevaut of France.

Welham recalls that at Hackwood the water feature for casting was a specially-dug pond with a plastic liner and a single wooden casting platform. It was the only time an artificial pond had to be constructed; from 1960 on, every Fair made use of an existing pond, lake or watercourse.

The Hackwood casting pool. Note the scorer sitting at his desk in the water.

Adverts from the 1959 programme.

At these early Game Fairs the split-cane rod still predominated and although plastic fly lines had begun to appear, the AFTMA numbering system had yet to be conceived, so most of the visitors wanted to know how to find the appropriate size of line for a particular rod.

Game rearing got a prominent role. The Rearing Field, as it was then called, was a focal point for the Fair, featuring as it did fifteen of the country's leading game farms. Clay shooting, muzzle-loaders, small-bore shooting, archery, falconry, a cinema show and a venison barbecue contributed to making the event a huge success.

Gundog working tests were in full swing, with an open stake for 24 retrievers, a silver challenge trophy and a guarantee of a £5 prize to the winner of each qualifying heat. It was even possible to buy a trained gundog or puppy at the show.

In those days of more formal dress, the heatwave led to some discomfort. There was a huge sigh of relief at lunch when the Duke of Gloucester removed his jacket, enabling everyone else to do the same. Nigel Gray remembers that sitting opposite him was an

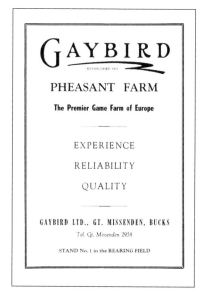

GAYBIRD

ESTABLISHED 1901

PHEASANT FARM

The Premier Game Farm of Europe

EXPERIENCE

RELIABILITY

QUALITY

GAYBIRD LTD., GT. MISSENDEN, BUCKS

Tel. Gt. Missenden 2958

STAND No. 1 in the REARING FIELD

Malcolm Lyell of Westley Richards shows the Duke of Gloucester General Tom Thumb's miniature rifle at the Hackwood Game Fair, 1959. (John Tarlton)

elderly peer who shed his jacket to reveal a pair of braces decorated with the images of nude women galloping up his shirt front and over his shoulders.

Total attendance came in at 12,000, a 40 per cent increase on the first Fair. *The Field* once again devoted several pages to a thoughtful report. It opened:

'Now that the congratulations have all been tendered and the success of the second Game Fair is seen to be a fact and not just an enthusiast's dream, it is possible to calculate just what was revealed at Basingstoke last month and at Stetchworth last year. First and foremost each Game Fair demonstrated the strength of the sport of shooting. [The number of visitors] is a telling answer to those who would talk as if the impetus had died out of shooting in their own early days and that the sport is now freewheeling to an eventual halt. There were few signs of this, and many to the contrary.'

The writer (presumably the Editor, Wilson Stephens), noted the high percentage of young people in the crowd; he reported that on the Friday, for every man over 60 there was another under 30, and that by the Saturday the younger group was two to one in the ascendancy.

'It may well be wondered why some shooting people have been so prone to talk pessimistically and why many of the general public had come to look upon shooting as an outmoded custom' the leader went on. 'The answer, in our view, was simply the lack of a Game Fair. Last year's successful implementation by the Country Landowner's Association of a practical, timely idea made many ask why it had not been done before.

'The shooting year has hitherto contained no gatherings, either locally or nationally, at which the shooting community could meet in force . . . [it] receded into a background which some people mistook for a backwater.

'The farmer trying to work up a shoot with his neighbours finds that his is not the only effort in this direction, and meets others who are doing likewise. The townsman with an interest in ornithology, who has brought his family on a rather problematical afternoon's outing, finds a new world laid bare to him.

'Britain has always led the world in game shooting. The Game Fair has proved that this is still so.'

The Duke of Gloucester (second right) at the Hackwood Game Fair with Lord Camrose (left) and Captain Bobby Petre (right). (John Tarlton)

34

1960: Castle Howard

Country Landowners' Association
GAME FAIR
July 15th, 16th
1960
Souvenir Programme
2/6

The unqualified success of the 1959 Game Fair brought a realisation that the communal spirit which characterises all field sports could be tapped into right across Britain. The CLA men recognised the value of highlighting, at each Fair, activities which were local to that region. For that reason, when the Game Fair travelled north to Castle Howard in 1960, grouse shooting was featured strongly.

This was the home of George Howard, who rescued Castle Howard from the threat of public sale after the Second World War and proceeded to restore and revitalise this great property, synonymous in the minds of many with the 1981 television production of Evelyn Waugh's *Brideshead Revisited* (the cameras returned in 2007 to shoot a new feature film version of the book). Mr Howard took a great interest in the Game Fair and was happy to sit as Committee Chairman; his wife Lady Cecilia was among the committee members, and took responsibility for the programme. Game Fair visitors were invited to tour the house on payment of 2s 6d per head.

The committee had swollen to 24, including ex officio members, while 33 stewards were appointed. Guy Beadon, Secretary and later President of the Durham Branch of the CLA, served as Game Fair Secretary (Major Gee continued as CLA Secretary at Head Office), and a W. E. Wigglesworth Esq. was given the task of looking after 'public hygiene'.

Guy Beadon clearly remembers the meeting in 1959 at Castle Howard at which he offered (after a sumptuous dinner) to organise the following year's Fair. With George Howard and the rest of the CLA team, he spent many hours working out a ground plan which would balance the various requirements as efficiently as possible. Although Guy is nearly 90 and no longer able to attend Fairs, it has given him great satisfaction over the years to see that the principles of that first ground plan are still being followed.

By now the Game Fair had more or less settled into the format

Castle Howard.

which was to prove so successful that it remains in force today. The number of exhibitors and trade stands had risen to more than 120. In addition to the spread on grouse shooting, gundog working tests were becoming more ambitious with open stakes for both retrievers and spaniels, though the scurry and its variations, so familiar today, had yet to be developed. There was, however, an auction of gun-dogs, with a guide price of fifteen guineas for dogs over six months, while puppies were eight guineas.

Tests for retrievers and spaniels were held in the natural arena created by the landscape beyond the South Lake, below Vanbrugh's Temple of the Four Winds. The falconers put on a spectacular display, though the onlookers were disappointed that the Austrian golden eagle was not allowed to spread its 8ft wingspan in action - the risk that it might bear off someone's small dog, or worse, was considered too great.

The grouse exhibit featured young, hand-reared birds (much harder to raise than pheasants) and a range of grouse butt designs.

Coarse fishing was introduced alongside the fly fishing, with a match pegged out along the shore of Castle Howard's Great Lake (teams from York and Leeds tied for the trophy). The smaller South Lake proved a much more satisfactory arena for the fly accuracy and bait-casting competitions than the previous year's plastic pond.

They were in part organised by that prominent angling figure Eric Horsfall Turner, a fly-casting champion himself as well as a pioneering tunny fisherman and a founder of both the Anglers' Co-operative Association and the British Casting Association. The contests included accuracy and distance events (to give the amateurs a chance, established tournament casters were excluded).

The banks of the casting lake proved an ideal setting for Fisherman's Row, now up to 19 exhibitors.

This was in the days when that fondly-remembered weekly the *Fishing Gazette* cost one shilling (5p), while *Shooting Times* was one shilling and threepence. You could buy 12-bore shotgun cartridges for 49 shillings (£2.45) a hundred, and Hebden Cord were selling keepers' breeches for £2. Those prices look less enticing when you remember that an average annual income in the early 1960s would have been in the hundreds of pounds; a London legal firm was advertising for a solicitor on £2000 a year.

The sun shone throughout, and 20,000 people came.

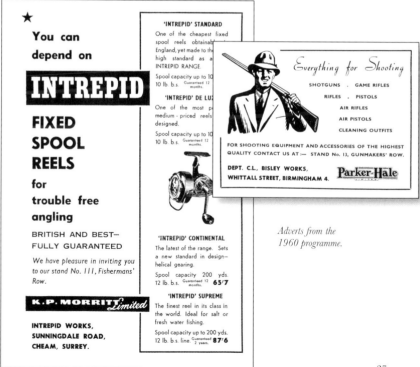

Adverts from the 1960 programme.

1961: Weston Park

Weston Park, near Shifnal, Shropshire, the home of the Earl of Bradford, lies only 14 miles from Wolverhampton, and is not much more than a bus ride from the Black Country. It provided a wonderful opportunity to introduce the town dwellers of the Midlands to rural pursuits.

The *Daily Telegraph* noted the Fair's status as a leading fixture in the sporting estate owner's calendar, while *Shooting Times* praised it as 'the Ascot of field sports'. With three successful Fairs under its belt, the Country Landowners' Association no longer felt that the title of Game Fair needed to be endorsed by the pre-fixed letters CLA.

Raymond Elkerton returned as Game Fair secretary, and as had become the custom, the hosting landowner, the Earl of Bradford, chaired the committee.

For those with long memories, the names of some of the exhibitors may revive personal recollections. Among the trade stands - now up to 120 - were to be found David Home-Gall with his excellent Double H pigeon decoys; Col. A. A. Johnson of the Priory Waterfowl Farm at Ixworth, Suffolk; Ian Crudgington of the Bath gunmakers of that name, along with Gilbertson & Page, Millard Brothers and Parker-Hale.

Among the game farmers, Liphook Game Farm, Warwickshire Pheasantries, Lincolnshire Pheasantries and the Gaybird Pheasant Farm were prominent. Gamekeepers were represented by the Gamekeepers' Association of the UK, which had been founded in 1900 and to which head keepers and single-handed keepers were invited to subscribe for 15 shillings (75p) a year, while underkeepers paid 10 shillings.

Grouse featured again, owing to the proximity of the Welsh grouse shoots, and a stuffed peregrine falcon and merlin, displayed as examples of the bird's enemies, caused indignation among members of the British Falconer's Club.

Family cars were advertised in the programme for the first time; the Humber Super Snipe estate was offered at £1225 plus a staggering £511 purchase tax.

Something of an 'own goal' appears to have been scored by another full-page advertisement, showing a young couple staring with dismay into a rural landscape which has been ruined by a new electricity pylon. The ad was from the owners of the pylon, the Central Electricity Generating Board, and protested that this same couple would soon be using power

which might have reached them via the tower in the picture. The message seemed to be - you want electricity, you put up with the eyesore. Public relations was less sophisticated then.

Shooting Times, in its next issue, gave warm approval to the Fair in general and in particular to its setting, but expressed 'dismay and

Flyer for the 1961 show, showing events from previous years.

disgust' about both the catering and sanitation arrangements, and warned 'Should (the Game Fair) lapse into a purely money-making concern and the accent fall on numbers attending, it is bound to spoil itself'.

Country Landowner had a warning. 'One hopes that the Game Fair will not grow so big as to destroy this intimate atmosphere, for the lusty infant spawned by the CLA four years ago has now reached almost embarrassing proportions' read its report. We were reminded, however, that the Fair did not produce a large profit for the CLA, because of the increasingly high costs.

Game Fair weather reigned once again, however, and attendance soared once more, to 25,000.

1962: Longleat

In 1962 the Game Fair moved south again to Longleat, near Warminster, by courtesy of the Marquess of Bath. The sun blazed down and the crowds poured in in such strength that the CLA was able to announce a new record attendance of 28,000.

Bob Arnold, as 'Tom Forrest' of *The Archers*, again welcomed visitors to the Fair while in the Main Arena the Pipes and Drums of the Military Band of the 1st Battalion of the Black Watch performed. Long-service medals were presented to gamekeepers and there was a falconry display, small-bore rifle competitions and archery. The trade stands and exhibitions now topped 130. In the words of the Marquess of Bath as he welcomed the visitors: 'The Game Fair has achieved the reputation, acknowledged in all spheres of country activity, of producing the best of everything in the most congenial surroundings'.

This was the year shooting lessons were introduced at the Fair, separately from the clay shooting. The Gilbey Horses ferrying young shots to the instruction area (Anthony Gilbey was a director of Holland & Holland) became a familiar site.

For the first time there was a parade of sporting dogs, while the gundog tests, organised and run for the second year running by the Southern and Western Counties Field Trial Society, comprised a 16-dog stake for retrievers and an eight-dog stake for spaniels.

This, by popular agreement, was the best Fair yet, as well as the biggest.

The Fishing Gazette at Longleat, 1962

Right: M. Lewis of Bath Angling Association landing a roach.

Below left: The Edgar Sealey and Sons Ltd stand.

Below right: June Humphries whipping rings on to an Apollo rod in front of an impressive audience!

*Above: The Accles & Pollock
stand with the famous chub
expert Bill Warren in the trilby.*

*Right: C. Summers of Bath
with a keep-net filled with
roach up to 1lb7oz*

*Below: Barrie Welham
demonstrating the 'catapult'
cast.*

1963: Burghley, Lincolnshire

The following year the Game Fair headed east to Burghley, home of the Marquess of Exeter and the Three-Day Event. It was to be yet another sun-drenched event, with crowds topping 30,000 for the first time. A happy, congenial atmosphere permeated the Fair, and the garden-party atmosphere continued to prevail.

As always, there were innovations. Among them was a display of more than 150 antique firearms from the collection assembled by Major Noel Corry from Blakeney, Norfolk and a demonstration of game cooking on the *Farmers' Weekly* stand - a feature which was to become a major source of entertainment over the years. Uganda Wildlife offered safaris – colourfully promoted on its stand by Princess Elizabeth, daughter of the King of Toro and a friend of Prince William of Gloucester, who had been on safari to Africa.

Under the uncharacteristically tabloidesque headline 'HE TRAVELLED 6000 MILES TO SHOOT CLAY PIGEONS', *Country Landowner* told the story of Mr Irwin K. Gurney, from Sacramento, California, who had travelled all the way to England to shoot at the sixth Game Fair. Others had joined an airborne party from Land's End, leaving at 4.30am. The Game Fair's magnetism was extending its range.

Looked at from a modern perspective, guns and gear seem mouth-wateringly affordable. A BSA Snipe single-barrel shotgun was available for less than £15, while an AYA No. 2 sidelock cost £92, less than one thirtieth of the list price today. However, inflation was on the march. The price of adult entrance had doubled again, to ten shillings (50p), and five shillings for schoolchildren.

Country Landowner reported that there was not a hotel bedroom of any kind to be had for 20 miles around, and that local inns had been taking bookings since the week after the previous year's Fair.

Long-service for gamekeepers had been introduced by the CLA the previous year, and this Game Fair was the occasion for the first

Angling through the ages at Burghley. Left to right:
Will Paton, Barrie Welham, Alf Woodcock, John Hall, Dick Orton.

presentation. The Duchess of Gloucester presented medals to 30 keepers.

John and Judith Head of the Barn Book Supply in Salisbury attended this Fair. 'I recall there was little if any catering, so a biscuit company which was there to promote a new type of cheese biscuit did very well from the visitors and exhibitors' says Judith.

'Drinks came from a flask or from the water tap. It did not occur to us to stay on site, so we booked into a hotel. Unfortunately there were so many people that by the time we arrived back on the Friday evening, all they could offer us was sausage rolls.

'Despite this, we were delighted with the Fair. We sold every single book, print and painting we had brought with us - even two bronzes we took to decorate the stand.'

Among the books which changed hands was a 1750 edition of *The Compleat Angler*, bought for a considerable sum by A. Norman Marston, the Editor of *Fishing Gazette*. He published a two-page article about the Heads in the Game Fair issue of the magazine, which sparked off the successful business in angling books which they still run.

The 1963 Fair saw the launch of another fondly-remembered angling magazine - *Creel*, founded and edited by Bernard Venables; it was much acclaimed by the angling world at the time, though it was to run for only four years.

The 1960s was a period of dramatic change within the sporting world. Men of understanding and depth of knowledge such as

Herbie Fooks and Arthur Cadman had been doing their utmost to get a better deal for deer. There were no close seasons and deer, particularly roe, tended to be treated as vermin to be killed or wounded with shotguns, often on driven game days when bird shot was in use. They were also still being snared.

The Game Fair programme had carried several articles inveighing against this cruel abuse. Relief finally came in the form of the Deer Bill (England and Wales). Arthur Cadman, then Deputy Surveyor of the New Forest and a leading protagonist in the fight for a fair deal for deer, wrote in the Burghley Game Fair catalogue of his relief to know that the Bill had received its first reading in March and that, by the time of that Game Fair, it should have passed into law – as indeed it did.

Out in the wider world, the Beeching Report on Britain's railways was being discussed in Parliament, while Floyd Patterson was still recovering from his 2 minutes, 10 second knockout by Sonny Liston.

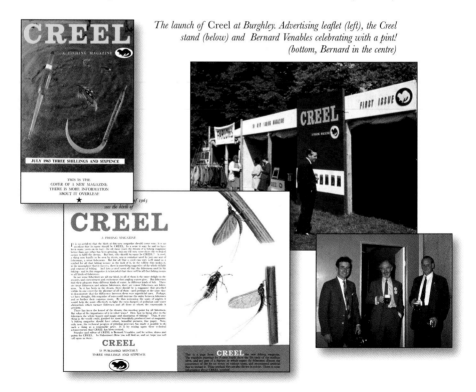

The launch of Creel *at Burghley. Advertising leaflet (left), the Creel stand (below) and Bernard Venables celebrating with a pint! (bottom, Bernard in the centre)*

4

Across the Border

1964-1969

1964: Blair Drummond, the first Scottish Game Fair

With six English Game Fairs safely under their belts, the organisers felt it was time to take the event north of the border. Accordingly in 1964 the event headed up to the 3100-acre estate at Blair Drummond near Stirling, courtesy of Sir John Muir, Bt. The Scottish Landowners' Federation, whose members owned some 60 per cent of all the land north of the border, ran this event, with the full support of the CLA.

This was the first Fair to benefit from the services of Brigadier Dick Keenlyside as both secretary and treasurer. A crisp and efficient military man, Keenlyside swiftly made his mark on the event. Few will fail to recall his peremptory but courteous Tannoy commands.

There was, understandably, a question mark over this first Scottish occasion. Would the Fair attract enough visitors, both from Scotland and south of the Border, to make it a viable occasion?

In the event, it was the first year when the admission figure went down, to just over 19,000, a substantial fall on the 30,000-plus

Left: Rosamunde and Malcolm Lyell with Sir Alec Douglas Home, then Prime Minister, at the 1964 Blair Drummond Game Fair. (John Tarlton)

Below: The Holland & Holland stand in 1964. (John Tarlton)

success of the previous year. There was some tut-tutting in the press. The consensus was that a lack of publicity, at least in Scotland, was the cause - along with disappointing weather; it was a dull weekend with spots of rain and very little sunshine. In fact later Scottish Fairs, though very successful, would show that Game Fairs north of the border would never attract quite the numbers that could be expected in the event's English heartlands. At least the Fair had won a large new audience, for most of those who did attend were first timers.

Grouse shooting and rearing, stalking and salmon fishing were naturally the dominant themes, reflected by the programme's front cover illustration of a red grouse. Exhibitions, instruction and trade stands linked to the three major Scottish field sports were organised by, among others, the Red Deer Commission and the Nature Conservancy, the latter promoting good moor management and providing scientific data concerning grouse stocks. Visitors could learn how grouse moors are managed and see live examples of all four members of the grouse family.

The game farmers were well represented, with some 20 farms, including three from Scotland. The 144-page programme was well supported by advertisers from north of the border.

Attendance might have been a little light, but this was a remarkably genial and happy Game Fair, distinguished for southern visitors by the authentic Scots sound of the massed pipes and drums of the 1st Battalion of the Scots Guards and the Argyll and Sutherland Highlanders, TA, who entertained an appreciative audience on both days.

Fishing, and particularly salmon fishing, was well represented, and the programme featured a three-page article about fishing in Scotland, written by Ian Wood, Editor of *Trout and Salmon*. That great gun expert Geoffrey Boothroyd contributed an article about the thriving gunmaking industry north of the border.

Youngsters about to have their introduction to shooting. (John Tarlton)

1959
Britain's first motorway opened
North Sea oil discovered

1960
Lasers invented

1961
Berlin Wall built
Soviets launch first man in space

1962
Marilyn Monroe found dead

1963
JFK assassinated

1964
Beatles mania hits US
Wilson elected PM

1965
US sends troops to Vietnam

1966
Mao launches Cultural Revolution
England win World Cup

1967
Colour TV broadcast in UK
First heart transplant
Foot and mouth disease -
    442,00 animals slaughtered

1968
Martin Luther King assassinated

1969
Neil Armstrong becomes the first man
on the moon
Hanging abolished in the UK

1965: Shotover, Oxford

Back then to England the following year and to the wonderfully well-named Shotover, an 1800-acre estate near Oxford. In the Middle Ages, Shotover was reserved 'for the King's pleasure to hunt therein'. Sport has long been associated with the estate. In 1965 there was still a driven pheasant shoot, along with partridge shooting on a reasonable scale.

The now well-established themes remained a fixture, and though Game Farmers' Row was somewhat reduced in numbers, the clay competitions increased.

There were also many more general trade stands. The foreword to the brochure was written by the Chairman of the 1965 Game Fair Committee, Col. Peter Fleming, whose brother happened to be Ian Fleming, the creator of James Bond; skill with words obviously ran in the family. Referring to the unexpectedly large crowds at the first Fair, he wrote: 'If anyone leaves the Game Fair with the impression that the Association's 39,000 members spend their whole time shooting, fishing, hawking, training dogs and disintegrating clay pigeons he will be deluded. It would I suppose, be possible to replace the Game Fair with something more austerely representative of the CLA's day-to-day preoccupations; and at least, if we organised lectures on tithe redemption, farm effluent disposal and methods of calculated unexpended manurial values, there would be small danger of the catering breaking down.'

As Col. Fleming wrote, it would be 'the mixture as before', and the result was another very successful Game Fair. The sun shone to order, and the crowds poured in in such good numbers that a new record of 41,000 was established. However, it was the first to suffer from traffic problems, with long queues of cars along the lanes serving the estate on both the Friday and the Saturday.

1966: Chatsworth, Derbyshire

The next Game Fair was hosted by the Duke and Duchess of Devonshire at Chatsworth in Derbyshire. This event was a spectacular success, due in part to the palatial house, set amid magnificent garden and water features.

A first-class sporting estate of 12,000 acres, with a pheasant shoot in hand, two beautiful trout streams (the Derwent and the Derbyshire Wye) running through the area and even a small grouse moor, made this a wonderful setting.

The Game Fair catalogues offer a unique spotlight on the social history and development of fieldsports and the country way of life over the past half century. Long-serving Game Fair people may recall Gilstrap's Game Foods, Parsons pigeon decoys, the 'Markor' shotgun from Cogswell & Harrison (£177.10s); Western self-loading clay traps; the Tryon Gallery and Wilsons' Dog Meal. You could even buy a Webley 9mm shotgun for £7.10, and if you wanted the latest in country vehicles, the Hillman Super Minx was yours for a mere £844.

Chatsworth was a crowning success, and great credit was accorded to Dick Keenlyside for his organisational skills, backed up by the usual enthusiastic local committee.

With an attendance of 48,500, this was generally agreed to be the most successful Game Fair yet.

Game Fair Types

Reprinted from COUNTRY LANDOWNER

Written and illustrated by John Tickner

THESE notes are intended as an aid to identification for the use of all visitors to the Game Fair and beginners in particular. Once you have arrived on the ground, look around and observe your fellow visitors, male and female, as you would any other creature of the wild that you might spot on a day's shooting, fishing or hunting or, for that matter, on a jolly nature ramble. Remember that most people can be fitted into types and that all sporting people almost fall into them automatically. It is hoped that the following information may be of help in classifying the specimens you see, bump into, tread on or are trodden upon by, during your visit to Chatsworth.

SHOOTING-TYPE PEOPLE. These will be present in large flocks, but can be placed into separate categories because the species embraces a wide variety of types, differing as much in habit as in plumage and ranging from the keepers down to the owners of shoots.

KEEPERS are present, as they will tell you, if pressed, as a matter of duty--a pleasant enough duty, of course--and they can be observed, lean, weathered, quiet, reserved, stalking silently around, casting critical eyes over the exhibits, especially those advocating 'new' methods, subconsciously being suspicious about anyone they note drooling over the pens of pheasants,

watching the dog trials, the fishing experts showing how expertly they could catch fish if they were really allowed to do so, and wincing slightly as they pass the falconry demonstration. The keepers have a most trying time at the Fair being polite to employers, friends of employers, prospective employers and even, when feeling especially benevolent, former employers. It is said that, once within the sanctuary of the keepers' own special bar, this type of Game Fair visitor relaxes and speaks his mind. But what he says is strictly secret.

OWNERS OF SHOOTS are much more difficult to identify than they used to be, either by plumage or habit. The loud-voiced wicked squire type, if he ever existed, has vanished for good and the present-day shoot-owner cannot even be conveniently placed neatly into one of two classes, the titled and the tycoon. Once upon a time, when the species first became split into sub-species, it was possible, the old men say, to spot a titled shoot-owner by his quiet, well-cut tweeds and the other sort by his more violently-coloured feathers. Today, however, the title and the tycoon have became so inter-mingled that the two are often the same bird and there is no guarantee that the tone of his plumage is proof of his origin.

But the keen observer can be fairly sure that the shoot-owners are the rather anxious-looking types going about trying to look nonchalant, being polite to each other and excessively so to the head keepers they intend to pinch from each other, even to the extent of buying them drinks when their present employers are not looking. They can be seen, many of them probably hope, studying the latest and most expensive sorts of appliances and devices to make their shoots profitable and trying to resist the blandishments of the expert salesmen who are there to see that they do not get away

without placing an order which will, in due course, indeed make their shoots more profitable. The best possible guide to the identification of a modern shoot is that he usually wears a mixed look of prosperity, which is probably not quite genuine, and anxiety, which is.

SYNDICATE MEMBERS often look rather more shooty than shoot owners, but this depends very much whether they come from a very shooty district or from an area where there is not much shooting.

If they come from the latter, they probably look very shooty indeed just as, we have noticed, horsey persons from parts where the horse is a comparative rarity often look twice as horsey as those who live in the saddle in the most 'hunty' counties.

SYNDICATE MEMBERS, if they belong to a big syndicate, are also to be found twittering round the trade stands wondering if the other members of the syndicate can afford to buy the latest devices to make their shoots prosperous.

THE CLAY EXPERT is not very difficult to spot. He is the man who has a slightly fanatical gleam in his eye and spends nearly all his time with all the other clay pigeon fanatics banging away like mad in a long line, amazing the non-experts with his skill and delighting the cartridge-making contingent who can be identified as those smiling chaps sitting on shooting sticks behind the shooters, rubbing their hands with glee as they watch the growing mountains of cartridge cases.

WILDFOWLERS are among the easiest to spot of all shooting types at the Fair. They are well aware that they are absolutely the toughest, most weather-beaten and most near-to-nature of all shooters and they go about looking as much like it as possible. Accustomed, during the fowling season, to carrying an extraordinary assortment of equipment upon their manly shoulders, they are inclined, by sheer force of habit to carry an extraordinary amount of items round the Fair ground. So, you see a tough-looking person carrying a gun, with bino-

culars, compasses, tide charts, cart-ridge belts, sanwiches, flasks and probably also his wife, slung about him, you can be sure he is a wild-fowling person.

FISHERMEN. Nobody in the sporting world can look more expert than the expert fishing person as he handles a rod in Fishermen's Row or nods his head in silent approval or wags it in silent disapproval, as he watches other fishing experts give demonstrations. Fishermen are present in shoals at the Fair but, ex-cept when they are gathered around the fishing area, they can be identi-

fied as those silent individuals, lurk-ing silently and individually in shady corners, as is the nature of their chosen sporting activities, ob-serving other types of sportsmen as if they were rather strange fish. Sometimes they are accompanied in their corners at the Fair by a tank-ard or a glass.

DOG EXPERTS. All shooting people think they are dog experts, but the top experts are recognisable at once by the top dogs that are leading them about or fetching and carrying things to amuse them in the dog trials. Never pat a dog ex-pert you do not know.

FALCONRY EXPERTS are a rare and very important species and are apt to be misunderstood by or-dinary and unimportant people who know nothing much about birds of prey. It is interesting to note that the falconers and their falcons attr-act a vast crowd of non-experts, all of whom seem to be able to recog-nise a falconry person at once. It must be something to do with their beards or their birds, probably both.

The great thing about the Game Fair, from the point of view of type collectors, is that all the sporting types think they can recognise each other, and, even more important, although they may laugh like any-thing at each others' particular fav-ourite sport, they do so, not only expertly, but thoroughly sportingly. Incidentally, if you do not think you look like an indentifiable type yourself, ask a type whose favourite sport is different from your own. He will soon place you.

1967: Bowood, Wiltshire

1967 Game Fair

Programme 2 6 The Country Landowners Association

Like Chatsworth, Bowood, near Calne in Wiltshire, home to the Marquis of Lansdowne, is a classic English estate. The park and lake were designed by 'Capability' Brown, while the house was built by the 1st Earl of Shelburne in 1775. The name Bowood was derived from an Old English word for a burgh in a wood, for this part of Wiltshire was once extensively forested; it was a favourite hunting ground for James I.

Yet again, Game Fair weather prevailed and the crowds poured in, though not in such numbers as the previous year. Now, nearly a decade after the first Fair, significant improvements had taken place. Admission was fifteen shillings (75p) and for the same money you could buy a cold lunch. Hot-dog stalls, licensed snack bars and cigarette kiosks were springing up. Toilets, still somewhat primitive, were to be found 'in all parts of the fair', trailer buses carried visitors round the site, and the press got their own refreshment tent.

The Gilbey Horses ferry shooters for their lessons. Game Fair Committee Chairman, Peter Fleming (centre), brother of Bond author Ian Fleming, with Malcolm Lyell of Westley Richards far right. (John Tarlton)

GUN SAFETY BY NUMBERS
or Ten Little Trigger Boys

by H. S. MORRISON

Ten keen clay pigeon shots
banging down the line;
one gun was out of proof
then there were nine.

Nine chaps out rabbiting
had to climb a gate,
one forgot to break his gun
then there were eight.

Eight tycoons came down from Town
to a shoot in Devon;
someone 'foilowed through the line'
then there were seven.

Seven sporting farmers
ratting round the ricks;
a trigger-pull was over-light,
then there were six.

Six cheery fowlers
in mud were said to thrive;
one plugged his barrel with it,
then there were five.

Five frozen VIPs
on a Yorkshire moor
'Unload the gun—like this you mean?'
then there were four.

Four crafty poachers
charged a hedge to flee;
no time to unload the gun
then there were three.

Three thirsty beaters
with a nice cool pint in view;
till someone fired into a bush,
then there were two.

Two farming neighbours
dazzled by the sun;
one took a low bird
then there was one.

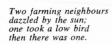

One veteran sportsman
loved his trusty hammer gun,
caught it in his watch chain
then there was none.

1968: Blair Drummond

1968 SCOTTISH GAME FAIR
Programme 2s.6d.

The second Scottish event was much better attended than the first, though well below the figures now being achieved at English Game Fairs. Thanks to redoubled efforts on the publicity front, attendance was nevertheless up to 28,600. The only major concern was the condition of the grounds; a hurricane the previous winter had caused a great deal of damage. The estate staff worked overtime to bring the estate up to scratch, with great success, and in the event the Blair Drummond Game Fair was a credit to Scotland.

The programme, still priced at half a crown (22$^{1}/_{2}$p), was packed with advertising and, as usual, carried articles by well-known sportsmen and women dealing with aspects of fieldsports and the countryside. They included a fascinating feature on modern stalking by that renowned Highland stalker Lea MacNally, whose regular contributions to *Shooting Times* were enormously popular. Lea was an observant naturalist whose life revolved around the year's cycle of stalking and deer management, first at Culachy and then at Toridon.

Other features included advice from the Earl of Mansfield, then President of WAGBI, on ways to improve duck shooting, while Bill Currie, a famous name from the salmon-fishing world, discussed the Scottish salmon situation, noting as an aside that 'people still catch forty and even fifty pounders, on occasion, and one still meets gillies on Spey

Caroline Lyell has a shooting lesson from Norman Clarke at the 1968 Game Fair. (John Tarlton)

61

who take over a hundred salmon a season to their own rods'. The country's salmon stocks were in better shape forty years ago.

Fisherman's Row, under the management of Sir William Gordon Cumming, ran a series of demonstrations and competitions, including the Duke of Westminster's Cup for a team fly-casting competition.

Both prices and prizes were still modest. Winners of the clay pigeon classes might walk away with a fiver, with £10 and a cup going to the winner of the Game Fair Championship. The gundog working tests, judged by the Wylie brothers, Andrew and Jimmy, were still based on an assumption that retrievers dominated the sporting scene, with prize money of £5 going to the winning retriever handler, but only £3 to the spaniel entry.

Above: Alan Sharpe of Sharpe's of Aberdeen gives Caroline Lyell a casting lesson at the 1968 Fair. (John Tarlton)

Left: David Shaw and Malcolm Lyell in unorthodox dress before breakfast.

1969: Stanford Park, Leicestershire

CLA GAME FAIR
Programme 2s.6d.
1969

Lord Braye's Leicestershire estate is in the heart of hunting country, so it was appropriate that in 1969 the Game Fair focused on the co-operation which can, and should, exist between game shooting and hunting. The county which is home to renowned Shire packs such as the Quorn, Pytchley, Fernie and Atherstone was the obvious place to introduce hunting as a feature of the Fair.

The organisers did not go so far as introducing hound parades in the Main Arena, but the BFSS did stage an exhibition claiming to show how foxes and pheasants can live on the same ground. An article in the programme extolled the need for shooting and hunting to co-operate, and the front cover carried a watercolour by Peter Biegel depicting the then Master of the Fernie, Col. Murray-Smith, raising his cap to a fox leaving Skeffington Gorse on a shoot day.

Unfortunately, page 24 carried an item which was rather less appropriate in a publication intended to appeal to the hunting fraternity; a full-page advertisement for the 'Hunter' humane fox trap. The Chairman, Col. P. H. Lloyd, was a Master of Foxhounds. He ordered

Casting expert Pierre Creusevaut with Rosamunde Lyell at Stanford Park. (John Tarlton)

63

the team to tear the offending page from every copy of the programme - 30,000 had been printed, so it took quite a while. Malcolm Lyell's wife Rosamunde remembers the sore fingers that resulted.

The advertisement for Cogswell & Harrison's Fieldman smallbore rifles which appeared on the reverse was an unfortunate casualty of this last-minute censorship. One hopes both advertisers got their money back.

5

The Soaring Seventies

1970-1979

By now the Game Fair had settled down into a pattern which it was to retain for the best part of two decades, and one which reflected the growing confidence and expansion of field sports throughout Britain. Shooting, in all its branches, was expanding and consolidating, carrying with it those industries which served it. Gunmaker's Row and Fisherman's Row continued to be the centre of attention, and even Game Farmer's Row was still able to muster in the region of a dozen game farms.

The Seventies was the decade in which the Game Fair became a nationally-acclaimed event, appreciated the length and breadth of Britain, and by country people and townsfolk alike. Success, however, was not without its problems.

The Holland & Holland guests at the 1970 Game Fair at Tatton Park. (John Tarlton)

65

1970: Tatton Park, Cheshire

CLA GAME FAIR

Programme 2s   1970

The decade did not get off to an auspicious start; the 1970 Game Fair was the first to be blighted by poor weather. It had been a good run, but the dice were bound to fall the other way at some point.

Heavy rain on the first day was followed by cold winds on the second. However, it seems a day at the Fair was far too important to the average punter to let a little bad weather get in the way, and in the event 45,000 visitors flocked through the gates.

This time the host was the National Trust, which had acquired the former ancestral home of the Egerton family in 1958. Needing a tenant to maintain and administer the estate, the Trust accepted an offer from Cheshire County Council. One wonders if in the present day such a use of a partially state-controlled resource would be thought acceptable.

Cheshire is a thoroughly sporting county. Not only does it have excellent shoots of all sizes, it is bordered by the Mersey and Dee estuaries which, in season, hold huge numbers of duck and geese and, as such, provided an excellent background to the 1970 Game Fair. It is a wonderful place for the coarse fisherman too, thanks to the Cheshire meres (Tatton itself among them) and the county's many canals.

The programme contains reminders that the Game Fair had by now evolved away from a purely recreational event into a focus for debate and action about countryside issues, particularly conservation. 1970 was European Conservation Year, and George Howard, CLA President, reminds us in his programme foreword that the CLA would have to continue increasing its 'already considerable involvement' in the conservation movement.

Judith Head, of book dealers J. & J. Head, recalls a particularly amusing incident from this Game Fair.

'We had just arrived on site, and like most ladies we immediately needed the toilets, so we left our husbands to sort out the stand and set out in search of them. No sooner had we found them and sat down than we heard the Tannoy booming - it was an announcement from the Game Fair Secretary, specifically for the ladies.

'To our horror, he was warning us that the seats in the ladies' loos had just been painted and were still wet! We had to get our husbands to rub the paint off with the help of pan scourers and scouring powder. They could hardly manage it for laughing.'

See Spanish Craftsmen at work

Throughout the Game Fair there will be an exhibition of hand-engraving and stock making on the ASI Stand No. C27 Gunmakers' Row

THE EXPERT'S CHOICE

HUSKY

S
T
A
N
D

B
4
7

ARE YOU AN EXPERT?

ILLUSTRATED BROCHURE FREE FROM
HUSKY of Tostock Ltd.
BURY STREET, STOWMARKET, SUFFOLK
TEL. STOWMARKET 2102

Tatton Park and some adverts from the 1970 programme.

1971: Stowe School, Buckinghamshire

CLA GAME FAIR

Programme 10p   1971

The following year, Stowe School in Buckinghamshire was host to the event at the invitation of the Chairman of the Governors, Anthony Quinton. The return of glorious Game Fair weather helped to make this a classic, and trade stands increased from 190 to 214. A record attendance of 45,300 delighted the organising committee.

Decimalisation was now in force, which makes the programme cover price of 10p seem ludicrously low - there had still been no increase since the Fair began.

This was the first Game Fair Sandy Leventon, later to become Editor of *Trout and Salmon*, attended in a professional capacity. 'I was a very young and very junior editorial assistant on *Shooting Times*' he remembers. 'In those days the Game Fair was still very much an amateurish gathering of fishing and shooting people.

Where friendly service still means something...

We are renowned throughout the South for our complete service to anglers. We sell a wide range of angling tackle for game, coarse and sea fishing. This includes several exclusive items such as fine hand built rods and especially designed Hay nets. We also sell clothing, accessories and gifts. We like to take an interest in our customers problems, so we gladly give free advice (we are well experienced to give first class opinions on all manner of angling topics) and pride ourselves on our personal service. Our repair service is second to none and is undertaken personally by Ian Hay. Please visit or write to us, we will be glad to help you. Or ring any time, any day with your enquiries.

The Rod Box

11 UPPER BROOK STREET
WINCHESTER
Telephone Winchester 61561   24 hour answering service

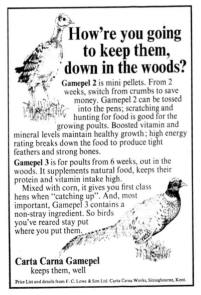

How're you going to keep them, down in the woods?

Gamepel 2 is mini pellets. From 2 weeks, switch from crumbs to save money. Gamepel 2 can be tossed into the pens; scratching and hunting for food is good for the growing poults. Boosted vitamin and mineral levels maintain healthy growth; high energy rating breaks down the food to produce tight feathers and strong bones.

Gamepel 3 is for poults from 6 weeks, out in the woods. It supplements natural food, keeps their protein and vitamin intake high.

Mixed with corn, it gives you first class hens when "catching up". And, most important, Gamepel 3 contains a non-stray ingredient. So birds you've reared stay put where you put them.

Carta Carna Gamepel keeps them, well

Price List and details from F. C. Lowe & Son Ltd. Carta Carna Works, Sittingbourne, Kent.

Obviously he doesn't read

SHOOTING TIMES
& Country magazine

By the 1970s, advertisements were getting quite sophisticated . . .

'The atmosphere was wonderful. Everyone seemed to know each other; tents blew down; demonstrations went wrong; power cuts were frequent and a wartime spirit prevailed. It was rather like a huge village fete.'

Stowe sounds like a paradise for the country-minded pupil. The 750-acre estate, according to the programme, featured a nature reserve and a collection of wildfowl, both maintained by the boys. Clay-shooting matches were regularly arranged between teams drawn from the ranks of old boys and local farmers. Young anglers could fish the estate's two lakes for tench, carp and pike, while trout fishing was available in a lake to the south-west. Boys were able to learn about woodland conservation and join the school's thriving natural history society, which was contributing regular information to the British Trust for Ornithology's annual bird census. An enlightened school indeed.

1972: Raby Castle, County Durham

CLA GAME FAIR

Programme 20p   1972

With Dick Keenlyside still firmly at the helm, the Game Fair moved north the following year to historic Raby Castle. Its host was the 11th Baron Barnard. Built in the 13th century as a residence for the Neville family, the Castle was open to visitors to the Fair at a cost of 20p on the Friday and 15p on the Saturday. Although for visitors from the south of England this was a long way to come, another new record was set, at 46,000.

Hunting in Durham was, and still is, a prime sporting activity, a fact recognised by an exhibition called 'The Fox and the Pheasant', organised by Captain Colin MacAndrew. This was designed to encourage hunting and shooting supporters to get together to discuss co-operation between their sports - essential if they were to co-exist successfully as neighbours.

Put yourself in our boots

You'll feel at ease

HUNTER
Designed for country wear, this lightweight rubber field boot has flexible net-lined leg. Calf fitting can be adjusted with strap and buckle attachment. Sizes 6-12.

BY **UNIROYAL**

Uniroyal Ltd. 62 Horseferry Road, London S.W.1.
STAND NO. G12

This Fair featured a major deer exhibit, reflecting the increasing interest in all species of deer and, notably, the park herd of red deer at Raby. A stall selling deer burgers caused a certain amount of comment; it was next door to one which featured a live deer.

The High Pond at Raby was the venue for a four-hour coarse fishing match, while the Low Pond, under the castle walls, provided a fine backdrop to Gunmaker's Row on one side and the gundog tests on the other.

1973: Abercairny, Perthshire

SLF/CLA SCOTTISH GAME FAIR 1973   30p

The third Scottish Game Fair took place at Abercairny, Perthshire, the home of Bill Drummond Moray, whose family had owned this fine estate since the 12th century. As was always the way when the Fair came north of the border, grouse and salmon dominated the scene, with an exhibition of live specimens of all the members of the grouse family, different types of butts, pointers and setters and even a pannier pony. Fisherman's Row was again organised by Sir William Gordon Cumming, attracting numerous traders and, as usual, including a series of casting competitions.

Deerstalking featured heavily, with a Red Deer Commission exhibition and stands dealing with the work of the British Deer Society and the St Hubert Club. Lea MacNally wrote in the programme that the rental for a stag on the hill was about £25, with a further similar sum for the carcase. He expressed fears that high prices for venison might lead to overshooting.

The gate entry at Abercairny was 37,000, a remarkable figure for an event taking place so far north.

The gundog working tests for retrievers and spaniels remained conventional, though the prize money for each type had at least achieved equality with a £25 award to the first dog in each section. Two renowned names in the gundog world, George Meldrum and his son Bill, the headkeeper at Sandringham, judged the retriever section, while Denis Douglas and R. D. Methven oversaw the spaniels.

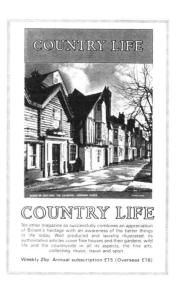

COUNTRY LIFE

BLEND OF CENTURIES. THE CAUSEWAY, HORSHAM, SUSSEX

COUNTRY LIFE

No other magazine so successfully combines an appreciation of Britain's heritage with an awareness of the better things in life today. Well produced and lavishly illustrated, its authoritative articles cover fine houses and their gardens, wild life and the countryside in all its aspects, the fine arts, collecting, music, travel and sport.

Weekly 25p. Annual subscription £15 (Overseas £18)

1974: Stratfield Saye, Berkshire

The 17th Game Fair was honoured by the presence, for the first time, of Her Majesty the Queen, accompanied by the Duke of Edinburgh and Prince Edward. Stratfield Saye, near Reading, home of the Duke of Wellington, proved a superb venue. The sun shone as usual for two glorious days, bringing a record attendance of 63,500. Unfortunately this is a well-populated part of England and the resulting heavy traffic proved to be a major headache, with long queues on both days. Even Her Majesty was delayed.

This was the occasion of HRH Prince Edward's first opportunity to fire a shotgun; he and his friend Christopher Wellesley were given instruction by Ken Davies of Holland & Holland.

This year of 1974 marked the beginning of a new era for the Fair, with the retirement of Brigadier Keenlyside after nearly a decade in

HM the Queen visits the Holland & Holland stand at the 1974 Game Fair at Stratfield Saye.

the role of Secretary. The new incumbent was Major-General Geoffrey Armitage CBE. Charming, forthright and enterprising, he brought a new dimension to the Game Fair.

Pugs and Drummers, an innovative and highly popular exhibition (the names refer to ferrets and rabbits), appeared for the first time, the brainchild of Peter Whitaker ('Petrel' of the *Shooting Times*). They are returning in 2008 for the Fair's 50th anniversary.

Another innovation, and one which has gone on to become one of the most popular features of the Game Fair, was a stand called 'Cooking the Bag'. A Cordon Bleu cook demonstrated novel ways of cooking game birds. It was soon clear the cooking of game was a popular subject with visitors.

Sandy Leventon, then Editor of the now-defunct *Angling Magazine*, tells an amusing story of this Fair.

'One of the perils of being a Game Fair regular is that the occasional bores which are found at every Fair always know where to find their victims. Our stand on Fisherman's Row was a modest affair, consisting of a smallish tent supported at its centre by a sturdy pole. The tent was square and bare, a magazine rack the only furniture. Since there was nowhere for a potential victim to hide, the tent was a bore's delight.

HRH Prince Edward fires a shotgun for the first time.

'One afternoon, out of the corner of my eye, I spotted Eric, signature briefcase in hand, strutting purposefully towards our stand.

'"Tell him I'm not here," I whispered to my secretary. Looking around in desperation, I realised that the only place to hide was up the tent-pole.

'Being reasonably fit in those days, I shinned up the pole and reached the top of the tent, so that I was hidden from view by the overhanging canvas.

'"Is Sandy about?" enquired Eric, already opening his briefcase, which I knew carried hundreds of photographs for my delectation.

'"No. I'm afraid he's gone for a wander and may be some time," said my faithful secretary.

'"That's OK. I'll wait," said the indefatigable Eric.

'And wait the wretched man did – until, with numb hands and cramp in my arms, I could hang on to the pole no longer. I let go, shot down the pole and landed with a thump, my face inches from Eric's.

'"Oh, there you are, Sandy!" said an apparently delighted Eric, and proceeded to hand me a sheaf of photographs as if it were perfectly natural for people to fall from the sky in front of him.'

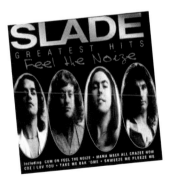

1970
Edward Heath elected PM
Voting age lowered to 18

1971
UK changes to decimal currency
Free school milk abolished

1972
Terrorists attack Olympics in Munich
Watergate Scandal begins

1973
Britain joins Common Market

1974
Health & Safety at Work Act
Harold Wilson elected PM

1975
Vietnam war ends
Sex Descrimination Act

1976
James Callaghan elected PM

1977
Elvis found dead
Queen's Silver Jubilee

1978
First test-tube baby born
Winter of Discontent in the UK

1979
Margaret Thatcher first woman
Prime Minister of Great Britain
Mother Theresa awarded the Nobel
Peace Prize

1975: Chatsworth

After fifteen English Game Fairs in fifteen different venues, 1975 brought the first encore south of the border. So successful and popular had Chatsworth proved in 1966 that the Committee decided to return there. Another new record was set, at 76,000, with 290 trade stands. The programme was now up to 160pp and cost 60 pence.

There was an exhibition of sporting dogs and Game Farmers' Row was still supported by nine game farmers or associated companies. However the game farmers, so long the backbone of the Game Fair, were increasingly finding that its date tended to coincide with their busiest period, and their numbers had begun to dwindle.

The Duchess of Devonshire was asked to make the presentation of the last .600-bore double rifle ever built by Holland & Holland, a beautifully-finished weapon priced at £27,500. Three wealthy sportsmen all wanted the gun, so a draw was held, and the Duchess presented it on the Holland & Holland stand to the winner, Mr Joe Wenger of Kansas.

As the Seventies progressed, the climate in which field sports were being practised and promoted had become increasingly uncertain. Coursing was under severe attack at this time, and Jim Callaghan's Labour Government had made it clear that it intended to 'deal with the other sports'. Naturally the British Field Sports Society was pleading for support and membership; not an unreasonable investment for committed countrymen, at £2 a year.

Peg making in 1975.

78

Tony Jackson and Matt Normington demonstrate taxidermy.

Peter Whitaker and Gordon Aveline.

The Pugs and Drummers stand and rabbit cart.

1976: Glanusk Park, Powys

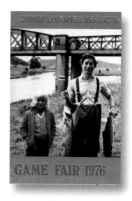

In the scorching summer of 1976, for the first time in its history, the Game Fair went to Wales. This was a fitting occasion for HRH the Prince of Wales to become actively involved, becoming the Game Fair's new Patron (the Duke of Gloucester had died in 1974) and visiting the Fair. Princess Anne was also present.

The event was a great success. Glanusk Park on the river Usk, the home of the Legge-Bourke family for 150 years, proved to be a delightful venue. Naturally there was a strong Welsh flavour to the event, particularly where shooting and fishing were concerned, and Fisherman's Row was well patronised.

Articles in the programme celebrated the almost unlimited opportunities for game fishing in the Principality and highlighted the potential Wales still offered for the development of game shooting. There were demonstrations of coracle fishing and the work of sheepdogs, plus an informative exhibit on the red grouse, arranged by the Hon. Mrs Legge-Bourke. It indicated that there were still reasonable numbers of the birds in the Brecon Beacons and Black Mountains.

The crowds rolled in to the tune of 78,000, some 2000 more than the previous year's Fair and, yet again, setting a record. Admission was still a modest £1.50 (50p for children). Catering and other facilities had expanded enormously on the early fairs; outlets for food and drink of various kinds had become

too numerous to list, and were simply described as 'distributed around the Game Fair'. The show had become big enough to need transport around the ground, and a tractor and trailer ferried visitors to the clay shooting area and back.

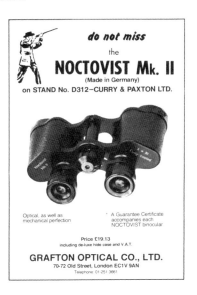

HRH the Prince Of Wales with Malcolm Lyell on the Holland & Holland stand at the 1976 Game Fair. (John Tarlton)

HRH Princess Anne took a turn at booking young shooters for lessons on the Holland & Holland stand at the 1976 Game Fair. She is chatting to the Marquess of Tavistock, who hosted the Fair at Woburn the following year.

1977: Woburn, Bedfordshire

Back to the English home counties as the guest of the Marquess and Marchioness of Tavistock, and yet again the Game Fair co-incided with a spell of searing heat. The fame of the event and the high profile of this grand estate ensured huge crowds, with the result that 90,000 people passed through the gate over the two days.

This was an innovative Fair. In the gundog section the International Team Match between England, Scotland, Wales and Ireland was launched for the *Shooting Times* Challenge Trophy, with strong support from Wilson & Sons of Dundee, the dog food manufacturers. The match proved an instant success and became the first of many.

Watching gundogs working.

The number of trade stands increased to 355, while the clay shooting lines now included nine competitions, in addition to the Game Fair Championship. There was a gundog scurry, a pick-up competition and a match between GSPs, viszlas and weimaraners.

In 20 years the Game Fair had evolved from an event aimed purely at the rural shooting community into a major player on the summer event circuit. Its supporters now included thousands of people who had little or no knowledge of country activities.

The Marquess and Marchioness of Tavistock.

Fred Groom with a 7lb catfish.

1978: Kinmount Estate, Dumfriesshire

SLF/CLA Game Fair 1978

The first site chosen for the 21st Game Fair was the Duke of Buccleuch's estate at Drumlanrig, Nithsdale. Unfortunately, on closer inspection, the committee realised that the narrow roads serving this pretty estate would never be able to cope with Game Fair traffic. Accordingly the Fair was moved to the Kinmount Estate, near the Solway Firth in Dumfriesshire, by courtesy of Mrs Edward Birkbeck.

Spectacular as this setting was, the ground available was not the largest the Game Fair had enjoyed and fitting everything in proved something of a headache. However, the Fair proved an immense success, attracting around 70,000 visitors.

Kinmount was a popular feeding ground for thousands of pink-feet, so it was fitting that the cover of the programme featured a painting by Sir Peter Scott of hundreds of pinks dropping into fields in front of Kinmount Castle. Alongside the usual shooting, stalking and fishing displays there were parades of black-and-tan Dumfriesshire foxhounds and of Capt. Bell Irving's pure-bred pack of Dumfriesshire Otter Hounds, then the only pack still hunting otters.

For the first time, French horn blowers had been invited to the Fair to demonstrate their remarkable traditional calls used in hunting and shooting.

This was the year Sam Whitbread, a landowner and farmer who was shortly to become head of the famous brewing company, became Chairman of the Game Fair Management Board. He was acutely conscious of the increasing size of the Fair and the need to balance its original ethos and atmosphere with commercial considerations.

'The business side was becoming increasingly important, but I knew that we must do everything possible to preserve what had made the Fair so successful' he says. In due course he stood down to become Lord Lieutenant of Bedfordshire.

Above: Mrs Edward Birkbeck.

Right: Donald Downs' casting clinic.

Scandinavian Game Fair

Horse-Hound Shooting Fishing Elmia Jönköping Sweden 24-27 May 1979

Scandinavian Game Fair 79 organised together with the Society for the Promotion of Riding, the Swedish Kennelclub, the Swedish Sportsmen Association and the Swedish Anglers' Association.

The Scandinavian Game Fair 79 an international exhibition with emphasis on the Scandinavian market area with exhibition of products but also practical demonstrations and shows.

The Scandinavian Game Fair 79 is directed at horse owners and riders, dog owners and people interested in sporting dogs, shooters and fishermen, landowners and fishing-water owners and all persons concerned with the activities covered by the fair.

FURTHER INFORMATION

Detailed information about the Scandinavian Game Fair can be obtained from Elmia AB, Box 6066, S-550 06 Jönköping, Sweden.

magimix
the revolutionary   French food processor

will be used by **Nicola Cox** in her game cookery demonstrations. Mrs. Needham, our senior Magimix demonstrator will also be present to answer queries and give you further information.

A copy of **The Magimix and Food Processor Cookery Book** by Marika Hanbury Tenison, cookery writer for the Sunday Telegraph, will be given free of charge (retail value £4.95), if you order a Magimix at the Game Fair!

Magimix is distributed by

ictc
25 Lower Square, Isleworth, Middx.

Adverts from the 1978 programme.

1979: Bowood

CLA
Game Fair 1979

The year 1979 brought another encore, this time for Bowood in Wiltshire, by courtesy once more of the Earl of Shelburne. The programme's front cover showed a group of Great Bustards on Salisbury Plain, reflecting the first attempts of the Great Bustard Trust to persuade these birds, once native to the Plain, to breed in captivity. Nearly 30 years on the Trust's successor, the Great Bustard Group, has begun to enjoy the first tentative successes in re-establishing these spectacular birds.

It was now that the Game Fair became for the first time a three-day event. Its Patron, HRH the Prince of Wales, visited on the first day. He and all the other visitors enjoyed the usual glorious Game Fair weather, and for the first time the attendance topped the 100,000 mark - in fact it soared all the way to 113,000. Trade stands and exhibitions reached the 400 mark for the first time.

Out in the countryside, not all was sweetness and light. This was the year Marion Shoard published *The Theft of the Countryside*, which condemned the catalogue of agricultural destruction which had laid waste to wildflower meadows, wetlands and ancient woodlands alike

Shoot with
the world-famous
Webleys.

WEBLEY & SCOTT

since the war. MAFF production grants and the all-powerful NFU drove the farming agenda, and conservation was scarcely discussed. It was not until the Nature Conservancy Council took up Ms Shoard's cause in the 1980s that this began to change.

Twenty-one years on from that first tentative event at Stetchworth, the Game Fair had come of age in every sense. Unquestionably the leading event in the countryside year, it was demonstrating an increasing appeal to the nation at large, not just those who participate in country sports. Its future seemed secure.

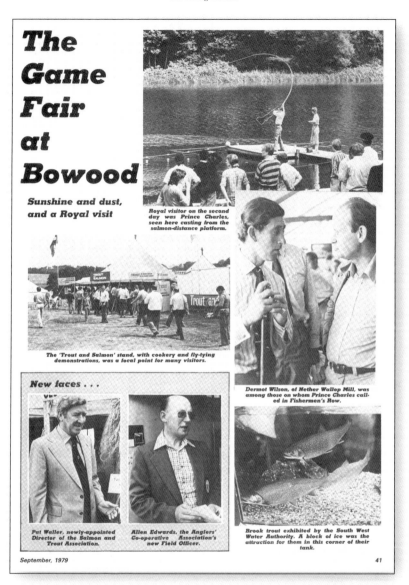

The Game Fair at Bowood

Sunshine and dust, and a Royal visit

Royal visitor on the second day was Prince Charles, seen here casting from the salmon-distance platform.

The 'Trout and Salmon' stand, with cookery and fly-tying demonstrations, was a focal point for many visitors.

New faces . . .

Pat Waller, newly-appointed Director of the Salmon and Trout Association.

Allen Edwards, the Anglers' Co-operative Association's new Field Officer.

Dermot Wilson, of Nether Wallop Mill, was among those on whom Prince Charles called in Fishermen's Row.

Brook trout exhibited by the South West Water Authority. A block of ice was the attraction for them in this corner of their tank.

September, 1979   41

Game Fair coverage in Trout and Salmon, *September, 1979.*

87

6

Bigger . . . and Better?

1980-1996

By the start of the 1980s the CLA Game Fair had become nationally and internationally acknowledged as the first, and still the best,
of its kind, and had begun to inspire others to set up game fairs of
their own, both in the UK and overseas. However, this was also a
period when, for a time, the Fair began to look as if it might become
a victim of its own enormous success. As the decade progressed,
there were increasing concerns - particularly among its core
supporters from the shooting world - that it was losing its original
focus on the country sports community. At the same time, by the end
of the 1980s economic factors were threatening to spoil the party.

1980: Welbeck Abbey, Nottinghamshire

The Welbeck Abbey estate between Mansfield and Worksop, the home of the Lady Anne Bentinck, commanded some 16,000 acres of Nottinghamshire and Derbyshire, so there was plenty of room for a successful Fair. The exhibition of 'pugs and drummers' (ferrets and rabbits) which had been introduced in 1974 was among the highlights.

This was the year the Fair committee bade a sad farewell to Major General Geoffrey Armitage, who had overseen such success as Director through most of the 1970s.

Although entry had now risen to £3 the crowds poured in, recording another six-figure attendance.

IF YOU LIKE HUNTING, SHOOTING AND FISHING, YOU NEED A VERY LARGE ESTATE INDEED.

Volvo are represented at the Game Fair by Ranskill Motor Company Limited. Telephone Ranskill 661. Speeds of Mansfield. Telephone Mansfield 643233

Lady Anne Bentinck, President of the 1980 CLA Game Fair Committee.

1981: Stowe School

As the Fair grew ever larger, it was becoming harder to find venues which were large and well-connected enough to meet its considerable needs. Accordingly, by the 1980s, fewer Fairs were taking place on 'pastures new' and more were returning to the established and proven sites.

One such was Stowe School in Buckinghamshire,which had hosted such a successful Fair in 1971. The 1981 event was the first under the directorship of Colonel Robin Rees-Webbe, who had joined the team from Riding for the Disabled.

The event was a great success, with well over 100,000 people attending, yet this year marked the first small reduction in the number of core trade stands - an indication of a trend which was to mark the following decade.

Gone was the flat daily admission rate. Prices were now graded according to the day; £4 for Thursday, £3 for Friday and £2 for Saturday.

An indication that not everyone thought big was beautiful is given by an article in the Country Gentleman's Association magazine which called the Fair a 'mammoth, mobile monster'. It went on: 'When it comes to the Country Landowners' Association Game Fair, members of the CGA are fairly equally divided. Half of them would not miss it for

John Taylor, Chairman of the Governors of Stowe School in 1981.

anything - the rest avoid it like the plague.' This slightly jaundiced piece is interesting in so far as it reveals some of the perceived negatives about the Fair at this time, such as the continuous noise from the clay shooting, 'the largest annual clay shoot in Europe'. But it concluded on a more positive note. 'The Game Fair is a chance to meet old friends, to investigate the possibilities of buying a new rod or a new gun, to admire the displays, to pick up a few tips and to drink everything from chilled champagne to warm beer.'

The piece discussed the great efforts by the CLA team, ultimately successful, to persuade the seventh lake at Stowe to hold water after many years of persistent leakage.

1982: Tatton Park

The Game Fair returned for 1982 to Tatton Park in Cheshire, again by courtesy of Cheshire County Council, with the Marquess of Cholmondeley as President. A colourful programme cover was the first to attempt to convey through illustration the sheer variety of activities represented at the Game Fair.

Helicopter rides were now a regular Fair feature. An angling video featuring Arthur Oglesby and Hugh Falkus was on sale at £29.95 (videos were a novel and somewhat high-priced form of communication back then). Among the many advertisers, familiar names included game dealers D. J. & M. Paul, Armstrong's Gunsmiths, Webley & Scott, BSA rifles and air weapons, Normark and Cambrian Fly Fishers.

The lurking threat to field sports was reflected by a BFSS advertisement in the programme warning of the danger of a ban on hunting and urging supporters to join them, while a flyer called on shooting men to join the CPSA (Clay Pigeon Shooting Association) to 'fight for your right to use a shotgun'.

Countryman, author and TV presenter Phil Drabble, Newsreader Angela Rippon and Charles Coles studying a Game Conservancy exhibit.

1983: Strathallan, Perthshire

This was the fifth Scottish Game Fair and the first three-day one to be held north of the border. As the opening day reverted to Friday, it was also the first to open on a Sunday - a handy arrangement for the Scots, as there is little or no game fishing or shooting to occupy them in their homeland on the Sabbath.

Sir William Denby Roberts' 2500-acre estate at Strathallan, Auchterarder, was renowned for its sporting opportunities, from stalking to driven shooting, while the fishing included brown trout in the loch and salmon running up a feeder burn below the Castle.

Mrs Thatcher had just been re-elected, and *The Field* reflected that the Scottish Game Fair had been made all the happier by the knowledge that the threats to field sports had consequently receded. However, the article pointed out that they had by no means gone away entirely and the good work being done by the then Campaign for Country Sports must continue.

Right: A stag on a highland pony, from an article in the programme by John H. Ormiston.

1984: Broadlands, Hampshire

The 600-acre estate at Broadlands, on the banks of the Test, passed to Lord Romsey on the untimely death of his grandfather, Earl Mountbatten of Burma, at the hands of the IRA in 1979. It proved a magnificent new home for the Fair.

Game Fair weather prevailed throughout the three days (Thursday to Saturday this time) and the atmosphere was relaxed and happy. It was hard to avoid noticing, however, that both Gamefarmer's Row and Gunmaker's Row had abruptly reduced in size. The former sported only a dozen stands compared with 27 the previous year, while Gunmaker's Row was down by 14 stands on 1983 - disturbing indicators for the future.

However, all the anticipated exhibitions and events took place, including air rifle shooting, clay shooting, archery, angling, game cooking and an extensive range of gundog events. In the catalogue W. & C. Scott was still promoting its guns and Major Neil Ramsay was still selling shooting sport in Scotland and Spain, while the London Gun Company puzzlingly announced that due to heavy demand they could not book a stand at the Game Fair - but would be in Gunmaker's Row instead.

Spratt's Game Foods, the rifle-maker David Lloyd, luxury gun cabinets from £430 and a new book called *Grouse and Gun* by Gordon Carlisle were among the numerous advertisers.

This was the year Graham Cox joined the gundog commentary team; his début led to an embarrassing moment. 'I had run out of things to say about a dog which was making no headway at all on one exercise' he recalls. 'As the struggle continued I let silence reign for what seemed an age before turning to my wife, Marilyn, who was assisting me in the commentary tower, and muttering "This dog is a bloody disaster!" Unfortunately I had not thought to switch off the microphone.'

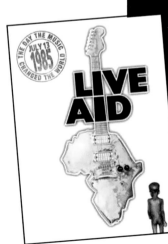

1980
John Lennon assassinated
Mount St. Helens erupts

1981
Wedding of Charles and Diana
New plague identified as AIDS

1982
Falkland War

1983
Reagan announces Star Wars

1984
Miners' strike

1985
Hole in the ozone layer discovered
Live Aid concert

1986
Challenger Space shuttle explodes
Chernobyl nuclear accident

1987
Great storm in UK
Black Monday hits New York stock
exchange

1988
Lockerbie plane disaster
Currie: "Most eggs have salmonella"

1989
Berlin Wall falls
Exxon Valdez oil spill
Students massacred in China's
Tiananmen Square

1985: Stoneleigh Abbey, Warwickshire

The following year the Game Fair moved to Stoneleigh Abbey, Warwickshire, the home of the Royal Show. The event was held not on the showground but in the spacious private grounds of Lord and Lady Leigh. Admission had now risen to £5 (£4 on Saturday).

The CLA President, Peter Giffard, surveyed the status of the Association in the programme, noting that it now had 45,000 members who between them owned 15 million acres of Britain (although half of them had less than 100 acres). 'The CLA is first and foremost a political pressure group' he pointed out, advising that at a subscription from as little as £30 (depending on your acreage), membership was an excellent investment.

Picture from 'The Plight of the Merlin', an article by Martin Jones.

1986: Harewood House, Yorkshire

COUNTRY LANDOWNERS ASSOCIATION
Game Fair
——1986——

Harewood House,
Yorkshire   £1.50

Lord Harewood's home, built in the Palladian style, is one of the most magnificent houses in the North of England and it formed an outstanding backdrop to the 29th Game Fair. This first venture at Harewood enjoyed the usual Game Fair weather and proved highly successful, despite traffic problems.

The programme covered a wide range of topics on field sports and conservation, including a feature on the Fly Dressers' Guild by Donald Downs, an article on chub by Peter Stone, an introduction to beating from David Leathart, a reminder (from Walter and Beryl Buckingham) that the muntjac was here to stay and a piece by Amelia Jessel on the flat-coated retriever.

By now the range of stands had expanded to cover every product or service which could conceivably be related to country sports - cookers and kitchenware, art, cameras and binoculars, clothing, camping equipment and outdoor furniture, basketware, horticultural machinery, wines and spirits, insurance and rain gauges. It was hard to see how the Fair could expand further without losing its focus.

Peter Stone with a large chub.

99

1987: Chatsworth

By the time the Fair made its third visit to Chatsworth, the numbers of both trade stands and exhibitors had begun to fall; for 1987 the number was 321, a worrying drop from the 400 mark which had been reached at Bowood eight years earlier.

The Game Fair's own success had undoubtedly played a part in this by encouraging competition. When the Fair began, open-air events for country people were largely restricted to traditional agricultural shows. By the 1980s, however, there were dozens of rural events to choose from, many of them with a strong country-sports flavour and some positioning themselves squarely alongside the CLA event by calling themselves (quite legitimately) game fairs. These shows, new and old, all helped to raise the profile of the countryside and country activities, but they inevitably competed to some extent with the original Game Fair for both exhibitors and visitors.

John Batley, well known as a professional pigeon shooter and now

The Duke and Duchess of Devonshire.

Director of the Gun Trade Association, has a good story to tell about this Fair.

'Falconry has always been a huge attraction at the Fair' he says. 'Jemima Parry-Jones has always produced a spectacular display, made even more colourful by her expressive language. When she discovered that her Rolex watch had been stolen while she was using the showers, she used the F-word - loud and clear over the Tannoy. A dreadful hush fell over the audience, before she recovered her aplomb to carry on with her demonstration.'

Meanwhile, there was change afoot in the countryside. Agricultural production levels across Europe had got so high that mountains of butter and grain and lakes of milk, wine and olive oil were making a mockery of the post-war philosophy of maximising production at all costs. Ministers, under increasing pressure from the young but flourishing conservation lobby, recognised that it was time to take a fresh look at the way we were using our green acres. A series of initiatives, notably a working party on 'Alternative Land Use and Rural Economy' (ALURE) of 1986, and a DoE and MAFF joint statement the following year on Farming and Rural Enterprise, set a more enlightened agenda - one which has continued ever since.

Labrador retrieving a woodcock.

The British Field Sports Society

Stand No. K980

YOUR SHOOT NEXT TIME?

... WAS THE scene on a ...byshire grouse moor on ...orious Twelfth last year. ...urs invaded private land in an attempt to scare the birds and disrupt shooting. Just one example of a very real threat to field sports. Other threats come from Parliament, local government and Europe. From biased media cov- erage and from anti-field sports indoctrination in our schools. From animal liberators and mis-guided protectionists.

The British Field Sports Society meets them all head on. Come and find out more about what you and the BFSS can do to defend all field sports at our Game Fair stand. □

1988: Floors Castle, Roxburghe

SLF/CLA
**GAME FAIR
1988**

Floors Castle £1.50

'Even in the sophisticated 1980s, the Scottish border country is a wild place' began the programme introduction for the 1988 Scottish Game Fair. The writer cannot have known how accurate his words would prove to be.

With a few minor exceptions, every Fair for thirty years had been at least partially blessed by dry and sunny weather; in 1988, that all changed.

This was the sixth Game Fair to take place north of the border, and the venue was Floors Castle near Kelso on the river Tweed, home of the Duke of Roxburghe. It was a glorious setting, and one which promised much. As the introduction went on to remind us: 'In these days of heavy financial commitment, the gate figure is all important. In Scotland people are spread more thinly than around a honeypot site like Chatsworth or Broadlands.'

Archery was very popular at Floors Castle.

They were about to become even more thinly spread, thanks to a severe depression approaching from the Atlantic. It hit before the gates opened, turning the preparations into the labours of Hercules. Then, for three nightmare days, standholders, exhibitors and a stalwart but increasingly sparse and scattered crowd were blasted by torrential rain and high winds. The grassy avenues between the stands began to melt into seas of treacly mud.

Charles Nodder, who was then working for the British Field Sports Society, remembers the 'Dunkirk spirit' that prevailed.

'The weather was unbelievable' he says. 'The only people who gained anything at all were the 4x4 makers, who could demonstrate how good their vehicles were at pulling cars out of the mud. To this day people remember what they were doing at the time of the 1988 Fair - the way they remember where they were when President Kennedy was shot.'

It seemed impossible that things could get any worse. Nevertheless, on the final day, a near-typhoon put the finishing touches to the tragedy by wrecking many of the stands and capsizing tents. Some stallholders were in such despair that they simply abandoned ship.

A useful vehicle for the Roxburghe mud!

1989: Stratfield Saye

Game Fair weather returned in force for the return to Stratfield Saye the following year. The sun blazed down and the crowds poured in, particularly along the M4 from London and the eastern counties.

While Gunmaker's Row remained relatively unchanged, Fisherman's Row had expanded to embrace 42 exhibitors and many competitions, including trout and salmon casting accuracy and distance, backed up by demonstrations in front of a grandstand by a team led by Arthur Oglesby and including Charles Jardine, Andy Dickinson and John Gibson.

The weather had returned to form, but the country sports community was becoming increasingly conscious of another enemy, one which would not go away when the sun shone; a growing climate of opinion among the non-shooting world against gun ownership and the shooting sports. This was the year after the Hungerford tragedy, when a disturbed young weapons fanatic murdered 16 people before turning one of his guns on himself. Many ordinary British people were so appalled that they were willing to back calls to ban private gun ownership altogether; the shooting world's reasoned protests fell largely on deaf ears.

The British Field Sports Society and the Council for Country Sports, chaired by Michael Colvin MP, placed urgent advertisements in the Fair programme appealing for support, while an article outlined the changes in firearms law introduced by the Firearms Act 1988. The Act had made a significant impact on shooting by restricting the types of weapon that could be held under the terms of firearms and shotgun certificates.

So the sport of shooting, along with hunting, was firmly in the public firing line. The Game Fair, now more than ever, needed to be the focus for an ever stronger and better co-ordinated country sports lobby.

The trend, unfortunately, seemed to be the other way. As the Fair moved into the 1990s, it began to be severely affected by the economic recession which hit at the turn of the decade. Commercial support from the core of the shooting world weakened further. Gunmaker's Row, always the heart of the Fair, appeared as large and as busy as ever, but many of the exhibitors were only loosely, if at all, connected with the shooting sports. By 1991 Holland & Holland was one of the very few major names of the gunmaking world still to be represented at the Fair, along with John Dickson & Son and the rifle maker David Lloyd.

The Duke and Duchess of Wellington.

CiBi

Rare Game at the Game Fair

TROUT *fisherman*

Stand No. H838

has the answers. If you're a bank or boat angler on the big waters; if you chase the running sea trout; if you tie your own flies – you'll find something to interest, entertain and inform you every month. Plus expert advice on fishing problems, tackle reviews, casting tuition, and the latest gossip.

AT YOUR NEWSAGENT ON THE 19th OF EVERY MONTH. PRICE £1.40

To discover the joys of stillwater and salmon fishing visit Trout Fisherman and Trout and Salmon at their respective stands and meet the editorial teams and their experts.

Stand No. H810

TROUT AND SALMON

Do you see salmon as the King of Fish, or as something that comes in tins? Do you dream of catching the hardest fighting British freshwater fish, or do you believe it's beyond your pocket? More and more people are turning to salmon fishing and finding it less expensive and exclusive than they had expected. On the pages of Trout & Salmon, on sale at your newsagent on the last day of every month . . . and enter a world of wild, windswept, wonderful fishing that could literally change your life. Order your copy today – price £1.50.

CiBi . . . *Stand No. C304*

Leather, Suede & Fine Fabrics.
Ready to Wear & Exclusive
Designs to Order.

49 Beauchamp Place,
Knightsbridge, London SW3.
Tel: 01 589 4361
772 Ecclesall Road,
Sheffield S11 8TB.
Tel: 0742 667815

1990
John Major becomes PM
Anti poll-tax demonstrations

1991
The Gulf War
Global Mobile Communication (GSM)
introduced in Europe

1992
UK suffers worst droughts since 1745

1993
World Trade Center bombed

1994
Channel Tunnel opens

1996
Mad Cow Disease hits Britain

1997
Tony Blair elected PM
Scientists clone sheep
UK bans handguns
Countryside Alliance begins with
Hyde Park rally

1999
The Euro introduced
Millennium Bug threatens computers

2000
Nationwide fuel protests in UK
'Right to roam' Act passed

2001
9-11: World Trade Center attacked
Foot and Mouth disease strikes

2003
Second Iraq War begins

2005
Hunting with dogs banned in
England and Wales

1990: Margam Park, West Glamorgan

The Middle East became even hotter than usual in 1990, thanks to Saddam's invasion of Kuwait in early August. It was very nearly as hot a few days earlier at the 33rd Game Fair, the second to be held in Wales, where the temperature reached 100 degrees Fahrenheit.

The 750-acre Margam Park, just inland from the dune landscape south of Port Talbot, would have been a delightful venue in normal circumstances. It is one of the most popular tourist destinations in Wales and holds the largest fallow deer herd in the principality, together with some red deer, Père David's deer and the last surviving herd of Glamorgan cattle.

On this occasion, however, the soft Atlantic breezes were absent and a prevailing wind from the factories at nearby Port Talbot brought a less attractive fragrance to the event. Andrew Young, who headed Browning UK at the time, remembers Margam Park as 'the Sahara with grass' - and wonders if the queue to the toilets has ended yet. Pigeon expert John Batley

says it was so hot that the tarmac on the Severn Bridge was melting. The local radio station was even advising Fairgoers from England to turn back - fortunately few of them did.

On a more positive note, Jemima Parry, the well known falconer, discussed the status of the red kite, whose last stronghold was Wales, and noted that an attempt was being made to reintroduce this splendid raptor to Scotland. Her hopes were well realised of course; today this splendid bird is numerous in mid-Wales and is breeding successfully in parts of southern England.

1991: Castle Ashby, Nottinghamshire

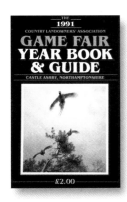

The 10,000 acre Castle Ashby estate in Northamptonshire, home to the Marquess of Northampton, proved a splendid setting for the 34th Game Fair. The house was built in 1574, largely in order to entertain Queen Elizabeth and her court. The park was laid out by Capability Brown two centuries later.

Eyebrows, however, were raised at one particular innovation; a jousting competition. There was a feeling that the Game Fair, once so perfectly attuned to its core audience of country sports practitioners and enthusiasts, was beginning to smack a little of *It's A Knockout*. Many of the visitors, particularly on the Sunday, appeared to have no interest in country sports.

The number of trade stands remained at around 330, but only 25 of them were in Gunmaker's Row. Game Farmer's Row (now called Gamekeeper's Row) could boast only four exhibitors, none of them game farmers. It was becoming clear that all was not well with the Game Fair.

Castle Ashby and the host Lord Northampton.

1992: Tabley, Cheshire

For nearly 30 years the Game Fair had been travelling the country from site to site relying on the goodwill and considerable free input of local committees. The paid director ran the show with reference to an advisory committee who met a couple of times a year. In 1992 an independent Management Board was formed, with a chairman and non-executive directors drawn from beyond the CLA's membership.

This was where the Game Fair started for James Gibson Fleming, who was appointed that year as Chairman. It was his task to review how the Game Fair had been working and how it should go forward.

'By 1992 we were in the later stages of a general recession and the Game Fair site at Tabley was not well known' says Gibson Fleming. 'The trade stands were finding it difficult to justify the costs of attending a Game Fair. We recognised that in future we would have to focus on prime sites that would generate sufficient gate to justify the enormous expenses involved in laying on what was in effect a one-off event.

'The New Board made an early decision to opt for fewer and higher profile sites, and to return to these sites on a regular basis.'

The CLA President, the Hon. J. A. Fellowes, reported in his foreword to the 1992 programme that the CLA had carried out a review the previous year which had confirmed that the Fair's objectives had changed. Two new ones had been explicitly added; to use the Fair as a platform to explain the place for country sports in the rural economy, and to show how landowners take a leading and vital part in the conservation of the countryside and its environment.

An admirable and timely step forward, no doubt. By now, however, there was an increasing feeling of disquiet about the way the Fair was going among those who had known it since the early years. The decline along Gunmaker's Row continued; the feature that had been the heart of the Fair since the beginning now had only 18 exhibitors, and not one of them was a major gunmaker.

Game farmers, once among the founder supporters of the Game Fair, were now virtually non-existent. The so-called Gamekeeper's Row had been expanded to include anyone with a tenuous connection to keepering, along with a cooker manufacturer, a power supply company and an estate agent.

Above: The host for 1992, Robert Armstrong, Chairman of the Tabley Estate.

Right: J. A. Fellowes, CLA President.

Tabley.

1993: Gosford Park, Edinburgh

The seventh Scottish Game Fair took place at Gosford Park, Longniddry, near Edinburgh, the home of Lord Neidpath. 'The event should not be seen as solely concerned with field sports' wrote the CLA President, Colin Dalrymple, in his programme foreword. 'Rather it is a chance for country to meet town, for people to enjoy themselves and for everyone to learn more about the countryside, about sustainable land management and about those who live and work there.'

The CLA fully accepted that the Fair should be addressing the wider world, but preferably not at the expense of a decline in its core support from the field sports community. Yet this decline was increasingly obvious. Forest Row was grafted on to Gamekeeper's Row and Gunmaker's Row remained in the doldrums. Only Fisherman's Row and the gundog arena, with its numerous competitions, seemed to retain the old spirit of the Fair.

The Game Fair in Scotland was still a five-yearly occasion, organised in partnership with the Scottish Landowners' Federation. Yet

James Gibson Fleming and his committee were increasingly clear that the economic factors were against this arrangement. 'With more than 50 million people in England and fewer than six million in Scotland, the Board felt this was not the best strategy, especially since there was now a competing annual Scottish Game Fair' he says. 'The 1993 Fair was great fun, but it was not profitable.'

And so it became the last Scottish Game Fair in which the CLA played a part.

Lord Neidpath.

1994: Cornbury Park, Oxford

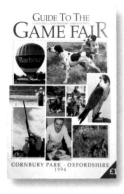

The venue for 1994 was Cornbury Park, Oxford, home of the Hon. Robin Cayzer and a renowned sporting estate. It made a fine venue, although many will remember this fair for its lengthy traffic queues.

This was the year the Fair switched from a Thursday-to-Saturday event to Friday, Saturday and Sunday, to reflect the wider appeal of Sunday to the general public. In fact the plan was to add the Thursday back to give a four-day Fair.

'The traditional Thursday and Friday crowd all turned up very early on the Friday morning and gridlocked the Oxfordshire road network' says James Gibson Fleming. 'The senior police officer was determined to instruct his officers to turn all the traffic around and send people home - luckily he was dissuaded!'

At 5.30am on the Saturday morning John Taylor, one of the newly-appointed non-executive Board Members was there to run the car park queues, and there were no traffic problems for the Saturday or Sunday. James Gibson Fleming had to write to 5000 members apologising for the traffic - but the Fair made a very good return and put the event firmly back on the map.

The programme was given a new look, doubling in size to A4 with colour throughout; it would keep to this format for three years. The gundog events were given their own separate programme, but the feeling prevailed that the Fair was now incorporating too many

1994
GAME FAIR

GUN DOG PROGRAMME

CORNBURY PARK · CHARLBURY · OXFORDSHIRE
Friday 29th · Saturday 30th · Sunday 31st July · 1994

exhibitors who had no connection to field sports or country matters.

Michael Evans had joined the team of casting demonstrators the previous year at Longniddry. In 1994, on the retirement of Arthur Oglesby, he was invited to take over the running of the casting events. He felt that an element of predictability had crept into them, as they varied little from year to year.

'I was very much a new kid on the block in '93, and I was most impressed to be rubbing shoulders with some of the finest casters in the world' says Evans. 'However, when Arthur handed me the reins I felt there was room to make a few changes.

'There are people who can cast fluently and there are people who can talk about it fluently, but it's very hard to find people who can do both at the same time. I thought it was time we looked further afield.'

Evans opened the Fair to professional casters as well as amateur, and invited prominent casters from overseas. This greatly enlivened the casting events, which started to draw bigger crowds.

Cornbury Park and the 1994 host, the Hon. Robin Cayzer.

1995: Harewood House

It was back to Harewood House, Yorkshire in 1995, this time as the guests of Viscount and Viscountess Lascelles. The sun shone and the crowds poured in. There was a strong emphasis on falconry, supplemented by heavy horse parades, jousting courtesy of the Knights of Arkley, a parade of hounds and a demonstration by Katy Cropper and her sheepdogs. You could watch mini quad bikes performing, learn about llamas and alpacas, invest in ostriches or try your hand at laser shooting. There was something for everyone - though not all of it had much to do with field sports.

Michael Evans' second year managing the casting events did not go without incident. 'We found the casting platform had been placed in the middle of a large reed-bed' he says. 'The construction manager was a coarse fisherman and thought that was the best place for it! He said it couldn't be moved, so I ordered a JCB and dug out the reed-bed.'

The Knights of Arkeley.

1996: Grimsthorpe Park, Lincolnshire

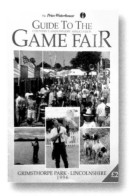

Grimsthorpe Park, the home of the Lady Jane Willoughby de Eresby and with a sporting history dating back to Henry VIII, brought the Game Fair back to Lincolnshire for the first time since 1963. Hot-air balloons, the Band of the South Nottinghamshire Hussars, terrier racing, cooking demonstrations and the 'Grimsthorpe Pageant' all helped to bring in the crowds, but there was an increasing sense of disquiet among Fair insiders and those who remembered the early days.

The number of trade stands and exhibitors had now fallen below the 300 mark - with not a single game farmer among them and very few of the gun companies. The Game Fair organisers realised it was time to address the problem in earnest.

The 1996 Fair was the last for Robin Rees-Webbe, who had put in 16 hard-working years as Director to bring the event through some of the most eventful years of its history.

'In the early days no one worried too much about making money' he says. 'As the years went by we had to become much more commercially-minded.

'I remember the raised eyebrows when sponsorship for the gundog events was introduced. The prize was a case of wine. I got a rocket from the Association for making it too commercial! But during the 1980s the Fair began to change very fast. The problem with starting to make money is that you can't go back - you're expected to go on making more year after year.'

He remembers that the cost of all the utilities when he first became

involved with the Fair was about £5000. By 1996 the bill for the toilets alone had risen to £55,000.

'The workload became enormous, and the local committees cannot be praised enough for the effort they put in.'

7

A New Lease of Life

1997-2006

By the 1990s, some of those who remembered the success of the early Game Fairs and recognised how well they had provided a national focus for country sports were beginning to grumble that the Fair had become too popular for its own good. The fringe attractions seemed to be growing at the expense of the core sporting activities on which the Fair had been built. Companies who had little or no connection with the countryside were riding the Game Fair bandwagon. And there was a concern that many of the people who flocked in through the gates left at the end of the day knowing, and caring, as little about country activities as they had when they arrived.

Against this, the world had changed, and the committee recognised that the Fair was going to have to change with it. In the early days, an invitation to exhibit was considered something of a privilege, and costs were hardly discussed. In the more commercial modern day, the event needed to be professionally and forcefully marketed. Exhibitors were, after all, customers, and like all customers they needed to be communicated with and made to feel valued and properly served.

Robin Rees-Webbe had retired the previous year as Game Fair Director, having run the event with great skill and efficiency for many years, so it was time to find a successor. The post of Director - always considered primarily an organisational role - had traditionally gone to a military man. In the commercial climate of the 1990s, however, the CLA recognised that they needed, above all, someone who understood the sophisticated world of commercial event management.

After a rigorous appointment process they gave the job to David Hough, whose background owed more to the world of boats and boating than to the countryside - he had been organising the London and Southampton Boat Shows and other marine events for a quarter of a century before joining the CLA. With him he brought Fiona Eastman to look after the marketing and show development. They were later joined by Charlie Benson to look after the site management, and Nicky Barr to look after sponsorship.

1997: Castle Ashby

To remain a viable and prestigious event the Game Fair was going to have to start growing again, and in the right direction. The success of David Hough's first Fair, a return to Castle Ashby in Nottinghamshire, would be a critical factor.

The news that a fresh régime was in place, coupled with sheer hard work by the new team, soon started to have an effect. In the months before the Fair, Hough's team managed to increase the number of trade stands from the previous year's 285 to 482, an increase of 70 per cent and the biggest year-on-year growth the Fair had ever seen. What was more, many of the new or returning exhibitors were cornerstones of the gun trade; they included E. J. Churchill, Browning & Winchester UK, Ray Ward, Charles Hellis, Chris Potter Guns, the Hull Cartridge Company and the West Wycombe Shooting School. There were also several welcome new or returning exhibitors from the game rearing world, including Briarland Game Farm, Bristol Incubators and Patrick Pinker.

Some of the leading UK firearms distributors had stayed away from the Fair for the previous few years over a disagreement concerning the CLA's stance on gun ownership. The arrival of the new management team provided an opportunity for the CLA to reach an agreement with the Gun Trade Association, which represented the gun firms.

Andrew Young, then head of Browning UK, remembers: 'We had something of a renaissance in '97, with the stands mounting displays of engraving or stocking. There were a few hiccups, but clearly things had very much improved.'

HRH Princess Anne.

119

HRH the Princess Royal opened the Fair on the Friday, July 25. The sun did not smile according to tradition, at least not at first - heavy rain had soaked the ground, causing a certain amount of sliding and slithering by vehicles. Fortunately the skies cleared, the ground began to dry out and the crowds appeared in encouraging numbers.

CLA President Ewen Cameron, in his foreword to the programme, took us back to the Game Fair's roots in one sentence. 'I do hope you will all enjoy yourselves during your visit, but that you will not forget that this Game Fair is a celebration of the role of field sports in the pattern of life in the countryside' he began.

For the first time a 'children's passport' was introduced. This invited youngsters to follow a route around the fair to find the answers to a series of questions - an idea which has now spread to almost every public wildlife reserve and theme park in Britain.

In recognition of the immense popularity of coarse fishing there was a much-increased focus on this branch of the sport, with demonstrations, celebrity competitions and a 'Have A Go' day, along with tuition specifically designed for children.

The clay shooting lines got a new manager, Neville Symonds; he would continue in the post for three years, until his expanding interests in catering - he was increasingly involved in supplying services to the Fair - made it no longer practical.

The Fair was in excellent health, but a reminder of the threats to field sports which still lurked at the gate appeared in the programme, in the form of an appeal from the Campaign for Shooting for support. 'A groundswell of public opinion based on ignorance has been persuading MPs that all shooting must be outlawed' it warned Fairgoers.

1998: Stratfield Saye

Like the Olympics, planning for Game Fairs was now having to be done so far ahead that the organisers needed to fix the venue not just for the coming year but the year after that, and if possible beyond. According to James Gibson Fleming: 'Our single most important job as a Board was to find the right sites, and this was becoming very difficult. We needed a site that was well known, and in the right place. It also needed hundreds of acres for the event and the car parking, and last but not least an owner who would welcome an invasion by the Game Fair!

'Consideration was given by the Board to having a permanent site, which would have great economic benefits and help us to bring back people year after year, but the Game Fair needs to visit different parts of the country. In practice we started moving towards having fewer sites - a trend which is still continuing.'

The Game Fair celebrated its 40th anniversary with its third visit to Stratfield Saye near Reading. James Gibson-Fleming had stood down as Chairman of the Board after the Castle Ashby Fair, to be succeeded for 1998 by the Hon. Richard Godber, who had been the Local Committee Chairman in 1981 and had also served for some years as the Honorary Director of the Royal Show.

The programme, which the previous year had been reduced to its smallest size ever - a pocket-sized saddle-stitched booklet - metamorphosed into a perfect-bound A5 book with a stiff, glossy cover and colour-coded pages, the format it has retained ever since. Gunmaker's Row now boasted a healthy 72 exhibitors, including such noted names as James Purdy, Boss, E. J. Churchill and William Evans.

This was the year the British Field Sports Society, the Countryside Movement and the Countryside Business Group joined forces to create the Countryside Alliance, and that spring more than a quarter of a million people had joined its first march to Hyde Park. With the threat to hunting in mind, there were parades of 20 packs of hounds over the three days.

Fisherman's Row also expanded and for the first time the Salmon and Trout Association organised the fishing events, as they continue to do today.

The Living and Working Countryside feature launched in 1997 developed further under local committee member Richard Benyon, now Conservative MP for Newbury. Located in the woodland area at the heart of the show, it entertained and educated a huge audience on how the the countryside ticks.

A new topical edge was brought to the Fair by the introduction of a series of seminars, with contributions from prominent speakers. The Lib Dem spokesman on agricultural affairs, Charles Kennedy, joined CLA Deputy President Anthony Bosanquet and Shadow Agriculture Minister Michael Jack to ask 'Is there a crisis in the countryside?' (unsurprisingly, the answer appears to have been 'yes'). *Evening Standard* Editor Max Hastings joined a debate on the future of field sports in the aftermath of the failure of the Foster Bill, while *The Field*'s Editor, Jonathan Young, chaired a discussion on the future of the Atlantic salmon.

1999: Harewood House

The Fair travelled north for 1999, back to Harewood House in Yorkshire. The site was much improved for this event by the removal of a line of fir trees which had been criticised in 1995 for dividing the ground and separating the fishing area from the rest of the Fair. Removing the trees fitted in well with the Estate's plan to return the landscape to its former Capability Brown design.

The Fair had not visited Scotland since 1993, or Wales since 1990. Many exhibitors found their takings away from the Fair's heartland were simply not enough to make their participation economic. In any case both countries now had their own Game Fairs.

At the 1999 Fair one could however see a team of Scottish lumberjacks at work or visit a Welsh Village, where exhibitors from the principality could see the best of what it had to offer - a great

Huntsmen and hounds gather in the arena.

success and one that would be repeated year after year. Teams from England, Wales, Scotland and Ireland contested the international gundog event.

Arthur Oglesby, who had handed the reins of the casting events to Michael Evans in 1994, was invited back to the Fair at the age of 75 to receive a Lifetime Achievement Award for 'the enormous commitment he had shown to salmon fishing, education and conservation'. The revered angler, ferreting expert and country writer Fred J. Taylor, by now over 80 and with more than 40 years of countryside journalism behind him, also got one. Sadly Fred died in May this year.

This was the year Steve and Caroline Penistone of Samsalin Dog Rescue were first invited to run a crèche service for Fairgoers' dogs - and mount a rescue watch for those carelessly left in cars.

'The '99 Fair was horrendous - I was checking or removing about 50 dogs a day from cars' says Caroline. 'With the work we have done since with the CLA in educating the public and putting up signs, we have pulled those figures down to just one dog removed from a car in 2006.'

This success has prompted the organisers of many other outdoor events to operate a similar service for dogs in distress.

A lurcher being put to the test.

2000: Blenheim Palace, Oxfordshire

The CLA Game Fair 2000

Blenheim Palace, Woodstock, Oxfordshire
Friday 28ᵗʰ July – Sunday 30ᵗʰ July 2000

Plans to take the Game Fair to Blenheim had been deferred in earlier years by concerns about traffic. By 2000 the opening of the M40 had greatly eased the problem, so the Fair celebrated the new millennium with its first visit to this grand estate, which dates back almost 300 years and is surrounded by more than 2000 acres of formal gardens and landscaped parkland.

His Grace the Duke of Marlborough welcomed the Fair with great enthusiasm. 'At a time when the rural economy and rural life are under increasing pressure, such a show of support and enthusiasm is of great importance' he reminded us in his programme foreword.

Robin Hanbury-Tenison, former Chief Executive of the BFSS, received the Contribution to the Countryside Award for his role in bringing together the sporting world to create the Countryside

Alliance two years previously, while the sea-trout expert and angling writer Moc Morgan, one of the most respected figures in game angling, won a Lifetime Achievement Award.

Following the success of the Welsh Village, a French Village was organised. Jointly sponsored by the directors of the annual French Game Fair and Veuve Clicquot champagne, it gave visitors a taste of life in the French countryside and opened a useful window on the many opportunities France offers for hunting and shooting, as well as farming.

2001: Shuttleworth Old Warden Park, Bedfordshire

In the spring of 2001 Foot and Mouth Disease hit rural Britain, and the Game Fair organisers had to think on their feet to save the event. It was scheduled for Woburn Abbey in Bedfordshire, the scene of the very successful 1977 Fair. However, Woburn is home to valuable herds of several exotic species, including Père David's deer, and the risk of the disease being somehow brought in by a participant or visitor did not bear thinking about. The CLA were determined that the event should go ahead because of its importance for country sports and the business generated for so many rural businesses. Accordingly, with less than three months to go, Game Fair Chairman Richard Godber, David Hough and his team set out to look for a less vulnerable location.

Charlie Benson, who looks after Game Fair site management matters, was the man who found the answer - Shuttleworth Old Warden Park, also in Bedfordshire, a well-appointed 500-acre park which had played host to several other big outdoor events. What he saw when he drove over to Shuttleworth and poked his head over the wall excited him enough to call David Hough so the men could take a closer look. They approached Hugh Duberly, Chairman of the Shuttleworth Trust, and Brian Welti, the Operations Manager. Both men went to a great deal of trouble at very short notice to help the Game Fair team turn the event into a success on an impossibly tight schedule.

John Batley, Director of the Gun Trade Association, remembers visiting David Hough at the new site a few weeks before the Fair. When he asked David where the car parking would be, the Game Fair Director pointed to a distant field of standing corn and said he had bought the crop as it stood - it would be cut green to make way for the cars.

This and many other problems associated with a last-minute redesign were overcome. Precautions against disease were installed, with driving through special bio-security washes to enter the car parks. This proved slightly disconcerting to the drivers of open sports cars, to say nothing of the motor-cyclists. Fortunately the weather was sunny and hot, so much so that vehicles were each day covered in a layer of dust.

HRH the Prince of Wales visited this show, helping to improve morale among the many who had been so badly affected by the ravages of foot and mouth disease. Thanks to canine passports, this was the first year when dogs could be brought in from Europe to take part in a new event, the Euro team challenge.

2001 saw the introduction of the Airgun Experience. This helped to attract many of the leading airgun companies, an area of field sports which was not felt to be as strongly represented at the Game Fair as it ought to have been. Another new area of growth was the Totally Food Show, evolved from the Country Cooking and Food show, which involved a series of demonstrations of fish and game cookery by prominent chefs.

The Arthur Oglesby Award was introduced for the first time, with a trophy commissioned from Ian Greensitt. A Lifetime Achievement Award for Services to Angling was presented to Anne Voss Bark MBE, well known in the angling world as a great champion of accessible fishing and a campaigner on countryside issues, as well as a writer on fishing and the owner of a delightful West Country angling hotel.

Above: A falcon on display.

Below: Fresh produce at the Totally Food Show.

2002: Broadlands

The show had now been strengthened to the point where the core areas - shooting, fishing and gundogs - were now each the biggest exhibitions of their kind in the UK and were attracting visitors from all around the world. The organisers were in a position to introduce new areas to the show, to attract a wider audience and provide them with an opportunity to learn more about the countryside and the role country sports played in it. Hooked on Horses and Elegant Gardens were introduced - and have proved a great success with visitors both new and old.

This, the second visit to Broadlands, attracted a huge crowd. They were able to enjoy innovations such as an equestrian area, a garden section, a new food area, an exhibition from the Royal Armouries Museum and even a World War II Spitfire, lent by the Southampton Hall of Aviation Museum.

Chris Green at Broadlands.

Broadlands 2002 was a reminder of the enormous size to which the Game Fair had grown. The expansive layout attracted some criticism from those who did not enjoy the resultant walking. Fisherman's Village, on the banks of the Test at the south-western end, was several minutes' walk from the heart of the Fair, as were the gundog events.

A Contribution to the Countryside Award was due to be presented to Dr Dick Potts of the Game Conservancy Trust;

he was unable to attend because of a family bereavement, so the presentation was put off until the following year. The great fishing writer and angling historian Fred Buller was there, however, to receive the CLA Game Fair Lifetime Achievement Award for Services to Angling.

This was the first year the Game Fair took to the skies. The Fair organisers hired a helicopter to act as their 'eye in the sky' and warn of any developing traffic problems.

The Countryside Alliance was now in full cry against what many saw as a Government-led assault on the countryside and all it stood for, and was calling on supporters to join its Liberty and Livelihood March in London, scheduled for the following September 22; a march which would be attended by more than 400,000 people.

2003: Harewood House

The summer of 2003 brought Game Fair weather in plenty; however it did not arrive until the opening day of the Fair, and had been preceded by several days of rain. Once in place the sun refused to leave, leading to a two-month drought.

Traffic had caused a few headaches at previous Harewood Fairs, so on this occasion additional parking was created on the far side of the A61 and a bridge built across the road. The camping area was much extended.

Among the highlights were a 'Village Life' experience, complete with village green and pond, designed to emphasise the importance of rural facilities such as the post office, school, pub and police station. Punch and Judy vied with a steam organ and a roundabout to recreate the traditional village atmosphere.

Polo demonstrations, a Fisherman's Forum, the John Bidwell shooting exhibition and an exhibition about horse welfare all contributing to a rounded picture of the countryside and its activities.

The New Countryside Experience was a new feature designed to introduce some of the ways landowners and farmers were changing the use of their land to make it more profitable, while encouraging more people to enjoy the activities the countryside had to offer.

This was the year the *Daily Telegraph* became the Fair's sponsor, and the newspaper was able to help spread the countryside message to a wide and influential audience. The Fair was the first countryside event to be sponsored by a national newspaper - further confirmation that it was now a 'world-class event'. The paper began by organising a hugely entertaining debate with a motion entitled '*The Archers* is an everyday story of country folk'.

Emmerdale *stars Georgia Slowe Sinclair and Christopher Villiers visit the show at Harewood.*

2004: Blenheim Palace

This prompt return to Blenheim marked the 300th anniversary of the first Duke of Marlborough's victory at the Battle of Blenheim, an achievement which so pleased Queen Anne that she awarded her valiant servant the Manor of Woodstock, along with £240,000 to enable him to build this beautiful palace. A rather more modest investment was needed in 2004, to enlarge the ground available to make room for the growing Game Fair.

Many first-timers were among the 130,000-plus Fairgoers, and it was gratifying that a survey showed that many of them had decided to take up a country sport as a result of their attendance.

The Totally Food Show introduced at the 2001 Fair had proved a huge success. It now featured an unprecedented range of fare and expertise. There were wine, whisky, cheese and chocolate tastings alongside the demonstrations of fish and game cookery. Separate stands introduced visitors to the Taste of Wales and gave them ideas on creative ways of cooking with children.

A cooking demonstration and Vinnie Jones taking a pot shot!

2005: Belvoir Castle

For the first time since 2001, the Game Fair now moved to a completely new venue. This was Belvoir Castle, near Grantham in Leicestershire. There was some concern that the maze of narrow country lanes serving the area would produce traffic chaos, but foresight and organisation saved the day. In the event, Belvoir proved to be one of the most accessible of the Game Fair sites.

With the magnificent castle dominating the scenery, the venue proved a great success. The Duke and Duchess of Rutland were very supportive, co-operating in the clearance of one side of the lake to make it accessible for the fishing events. The well-stocked lake also allowed coarse fishing to be highlighted.

Food was again a dominant theme, with the launch by Hugh Fearnley-Whittingstall of the CLA Food Chain Initiative. A greatly expanded Regional Food Court featured many more regional food producers, along with demonstrations of cooking by seven leading chefs.

This was the last Game Fair for the Hon. Richard Godber, who took over as Chairman of the Game Fair Management Board from James Gibson Fleming after the Castle Ashby Fair in 1997. Richard had guided the Game Fair with a sure hand through a period of great change. He had been particularly strong in ensuring that the Fair gave everyone an equal opportunity to promote their area of Country Sports, or as Richard put it 'providing a level playing field'.

Richard's unflappable approach made him the ideal Chairman for a team which was frequently under extreme pressure as a result of issues outside its control, from weather to disease. Napoleon said he always valued such generals - Richard's record of Game Fair's weather would have made him very popular with Bonaparte. During Richard's eight years as Chairman the Fair grew enormously, with both visitors and exhibitor numbers greatly increased.

Richard Godber was succeeded for 2006 by Vincent Hedley Lewis, who had been the Local Chairman in 2001, the traumatic year of Foot and Mouth.

Clockwise from top left:

Seasonal produce.

Jeremy Paxman.

Fishing at Belvoir.

Meeting a ferret.

Muzzle loaders on display.

2006: Broadlands

Careful organisation and the creation of a new vehicle entrance to the ground improved the traffic flow at Broadlands in 2006, although a major road accident a few miles from the ground blocked some routes on the Friday and caused long delays. Following the lessons of the 2002 Fair, the site layout was changed to reduce some of the walking distances, and a new area was opened up on the far side of the river Test.

Game Fair Radio, run by Airwaves, was now broadcasting 24 hours a day throughout the Fair, supplying traffic and parking updates, event information, celebrity news and the latest on the weather - and there was no uncertainty about that at the 2006 Fair - the sun beat down throughout, helping ticket sales to reach a new record of 138,000. No one seemed to be deterred by the entrance fees, which had unavoidably had to rise to cover the enormous costs of putting on the event.

The following February all who were involved with the Fair were saddened by the news that Sir John Ruggles-Brise, the man who had had the foresight to recommend the CLA's backing for the first Game Fair back in 1958, had died. He was 98.

2007: 'Cancelling Christmas'

After nearly half a century of unbroken success (barring occasional skirmishes with the rain-clouds and the traffic), the CLA and the Game Fair team were looking forward to the 50th Game Fair at Harewood House in July 2007. Unfortunately, there were greater forces at work.

The jet stream which brings our British weather had moved further south than usual, carrying saturated air from the tropics to the UK's doorstep instead of safely to the north. The sunshine which had smiled on almost every Game Fair since its inception vanished for most of the summer, to be replaced by the wettest weather most people could remember. Throughout June and July waxproofs were a daily requirement, while sunglasses gathered dust in drawers.

The rainfall reached a climax on July 20, the Friday before the planned Fair. In places, 50mm (two inches) fell in an hour. Very heavy rain is one thing - persistent very heavy rain is another. This was no isolated thundershower but what the forecasters sometimes rather entertainingly call 'organised' rainfall; on July 20, several English counties recorded levels of more than 100mm in 24 hours.

The Game Fair team were considerably more organised than the rainfall - they had put in trackway and barkchip roads - but at the eleventh hour, despite all their planning, they had to admit that to go ahead would be impossible. The site was slowly turning into a lake, and yet more rain was forecast.

On Sunday July 22, the CLA made the difficult decision that there was no option but to cancel the show for the first time in its history. The cost to the CLA and all the exhibitors and sponsors was enormous, while the cost in terms of lost spending by visitors was put at £50 million - £12m inside the show, plus £38m in the surrounding region.

The Chairman of the Game Fair Board, Vincent Hedley Lewis, issued a statement. 'Our hearts go out to all the people whose livelihood is going to be affected' he said. 'We have truly done all we could to keep the show going for everyone's sake. To proceed this week, with the impossibly wet conditions we are experiencing, would be a health and safety risk, and would create an even greater financial loss for the hundreds of businesses and individuals who are part of our event.

'We were not defeated by foot and mouth in 2001, but the rain has defeated us this summer.'

Shooting Times commented: 'The organisers of the CLA Game Fair are certainly in our thoughts today. It's a devastating decision they've been forced to take - devastating for the field sports fans who rely on the Fair to keep the spirit of their community alive, devastating for the exhibitors for whom the show is the highlight of a busy show season and a major financial investment, devastating for the local community, the hotels, the pubs, the shops, for whom the influx of visitors means welcome business.

'It is heart-breaking to think that all the time and energy so many people spend in preparation for the highlight of the summer calendar can be washed away like this. In the field sports world, it's like cancelling Christmas.'

It was a devastating disappointment for everyone involved with the Fair, not least the Local Committee Chairman, Christopher Bourne Arton, and his voluntary committee, who had all put so much into organising the event.

The centenary celebrations would have to wait another year.

Harewood, July 22, 2007.

8

The Game Fair at 50

The event that began life with an informal conversation between two game-rearing specialists more than half a century ago has today metamorphosed into an operation so complex, so sophisticated and so professional that Charles Coles and Nigel Gray would scarcely recognise it.

But perhaps that is a superficial judgement. Look beneath the intensely commercial operation the Game Fair has become and you still see the same fundamental driving forces; the fellowship, the sense of community and the deep love of country activities that set a fire under the Fair when it began in 1958.

Charles is still with us of course, at a sprightly 90, though he has not attended a Fair for some years. He still finds it a source of great pride that the event has gone on to such greatness.

As this book headed for the presses in June, most of the preparations for the 2008 Game Fair had long since been made. Blenheim Palace was confirmed as the venue four years ago.

'The first job is to select the site' says Vincent Hedley Lewis, CLA Board Member and Chairman of the Game Fair Management Board since 2006. 'This needs to be done years in advance, because the ground has to be prepared and in many instances additional areas put into grass. Then the infrastructure must be put in.'

The site must have at least 500 acres to accommodate the show, the caravan and campsite and the car parks. It has to be attractive, appealing and in a convenient part of the country, preferably within reach of the major population concentrations. A good local road system, with plenty of access to the property, is essential. There must be water for the fishing, rough ground for the gundog events and an area where the clay line can operate effectively and safely. Few estates have enough land already under grass, so usually, in the year leading up to the event, a suitable area is cleared and seeded.

Once the venue has been fixed, the team must investigate a myriad logistical issues. They need access to mains water and a means of disposing of tons of rubbish and many gallons of wet waste - the show uses more water and generates more waste per day than a good-sized town. The CLA now owns enormous storage tanks capable of holding 47,000 gallons of water and storing a similar amount of wet waste before disposal.

The layout of each show is individually planned. If it's a new site, or one that hasn't been used for some time, this is quite a challenge. The Fair must be made to work properly as an event regardless of the contours, walls, fences, woods, trees, watercourses, ha-has and other features of the landscape.

With more than 23,000 vehicles coming in to the showground each day, traffic planning is critical. The details are discussed in detail with the police, the local authorities and the Highway Agency to make sure nothing is left to chance. During the show itself, a dedicated traffic control team enjoys the services of the Game Fair's own helicopter, with a TV downlink, which enables them to spot any hold-ups quickly and activate alternative routes.

Then there are the many services and equipment the Fair buys in from outside suppliers - umpteen acres of tentage, miles of fencing, dozens of portable cabins and toilet units. An army of people must be recruited to supervise car parking, operate the gates, keep the site clean, look after First Aid and lay on electricity (the electrical supply to the Fair requires 55 generators and 18 miles of cables).

It is hard for an outsider to appreciate just how much work is involved, and how many people are needed to do it.

'Over the years we have seen the Game Fair grow into an enormous event' says James Gibson Fleming. 'The Local Committees do a huge job as volunteers and still don't get full credit for all they do. What has changed is the amount of professional input needed, and the massive infrastructure required.

'It has always been the great platform for the field sports industry. The challenge remains to maintain this platform, but to keep moving forward.'

Catering facilities are always under great pressure. The goalposts have moved a little since that first event 50 years ago at Stetchworth, when a single desperately over-subscribed kitchen struggled to cope with a mere 4000 people a day, less than a tenth of today's figure. During the three days of a modern Fair, some 13,000 glasses of Pimms, 86,000 cups of coffee and countless barrels of beer and lager are dispensed by the caterers - and that's for the CLA Members' Enclosure alone. The choicest parts of 340 pigs and nearly a tonne of smoked salmon are served, to say nothing of vast quantities of soft drinks, ices, snacks and ready meals from cuisines around the world. Around the Fair, site catering units are encouraged to serve local and regional produce. The caterers looking after the Members' Enclosure are contracted to source their supplies, where possible, from the local area.

The job of allocating space to around a thousand exhibitors is always challenging. Placing each one in the right part of the Fair is just the start. Several other factors have to be taken into account, such as requests for corner stands, or the desire of some companies to exhibit alongside one another or close to particular facilities. While the organisers try to put the needs of long-established Fair supporters first, they also do their best to encourage and accommodate the new exhibitors.

The work on site starts around the beginning of June, when the site team and an army of contractors move in. Very soon a small town has sprung up to house them all; some will be spending three months on site.

Piping and cables have to go in, toilets must be installed, marquees and tents erected and temporary fences, bridges and pontoons put up (and permanent ones removed). New entrances have to be constructed and a network of internal 'roads' put in. There may be acres of grass to be cut, along with trees and scrub to be cleared.

A week before the Fair, the exhibitors will start arriving to prepare their stands. Vans, lorries, pick-ups, four-wheel drives, horseboxes, dog trailers, refrigerated containers - all have to be marshalled into position and connected to power supplies. At last, on the eve of the Fair, everything is ready.

Dawn on the first day is a time of great anticipation. Curtains are drawn and windows thrown open as exhibitors, organisers, staff, all those involved with the Fair, look out on the day to see if the sun has answered their prayers. The opening of this unique shop window on the countryside brings a rush of adrenalin for everyone, from the Game Fair team and Board to the volunteers and the youngsters who have been working hard for the past six weeks to prepare the site. When the gates finally open on the Friday morning, it's a very special moment.

For the Broadlands Game Fair in 2006, I decided to bring my accommodation with me in the shape of a mobile home. The Caravan Club, with which I have a formal and close relationship, kindly loaned me a superb vehicle for my stay at the Fair. And bingo! My commuting days were over. All we did was close the Middle Way Group stand at the end of the day and travel about five feet to our mobile abode.

Just to underline the prudence of staying on site, and with immaculate timing, a story appeared in the Daily Telegraph *on the opening day of the Fair, which led to us being involved with radio interviews for most of the afternoon. Just as we'd finished, a BBC reporter invited us to participate in a live debate at 12 midnight! Not the best time, but who are we to turn down such an offer? The Game Fair press office even made the radio link-up available, without which we'd have been free to enjoy our whole night. Thanks guys . . .*

With plenty of time to eat before the programme, a group of us decided to go off to a Romsey curry house. On our return, we found the gate locked! The hubris of being so smug about our mobile home was biting where it hurt. Like the seasoned media veterans we were, we thought for a while . . . and then panicked.

Finally, we decided to ease our way very carefully, in total darkness, over a barbed-wire-fenced gate. We reached the press room and completed the interview. Jim had a scar where it REALLY hurt for a week. But the mobile home is here to stay.

Lembit Opik, Lib Dem MP

By midday the grass-and-canvas landscape which a few hours

earlier had woken to the first rays of the dawn sun has become a cheerful riot of colour and noise. Smartly-dressed sporting types in panama hats stroll proprietorially among the field sports areas. Families with pushchairs try to take in as much as they can of the Fair in between pacifying their suncream-smothered broods. Perspiring youngsters in T-shirts slave over hot griddles to appease the long queue that has been lured by the smell of burgers and fried onions. Couples flirt among the stands, modelling country coats and silly hats for each other. Fashionable women shop, with shooting sticks and deadly purpose. Red-faced men in shooting vests, gunslips slung at one o'clock, march resolutely towards the sound of artillery. Family parties sprawl on the grass with soft drinks and coolboxes. The loudspeakers relay the measured tones of a casting magician as he begins his daily performance down on the jetty, and the crowd by the lake, anglers and innocents alike, gawp in astonishment as they watch his rod and line defying the laws of physics.

It has all changed enormously, and yet it hasn't. While the Game Fair has grown and moved with the times, it is still essentially a joyful gathering of country-lovers revelling in all that's great about Britain and its rich sporting heritage.

The variety of entertainments and distractions is breathtaking. It is as if everything that ever happens in the countryside has been pulled together into one spot for three days, like those old-fashioned paintings of nature that show an impossible variety of plants, birds and animals all sharing the same six-by-four woodland glade. The real countryside, one imagines, must have been left quite deserted.

The hardcore sportsman still makes a beeline for Gunmaker's Row or Fisherman's Row, both of which have grown so much in size and stature over the years, while wives and girlfriends spend happy and extravagant hours browsing the food halls and trying the latest country fashions. Very often it's the other way round of course, and it's the men who look on in admiration as their partners cast or swing with deadly precision.

The greatest strength of the Game Fair is its democratic approach to the activities it promotes - there is no sense of 'them and us'. For some it is a business opportunity, for others a chance to see the latest developments in sporting equipment or to indulge in three days of gundogs and everything to do with them. For many, it is simply a wonderful chance to go shopping.

Where have all the big walking-sticks gone? Twenty-five years ago, at my first Game Fair, they formed a strolling spinney, almost a Birnam forest come to Dunsinane. They were wielded by the big characters of the countryside, men like John Anderton of WAGBI (later BASC) and John Phillips of what was to become the Heather Trust. They were a badge of office, worn like a French noble-man's dress sword before that appointment with Madame Guillotine.

Other Game Fair castes had their own unmistakable plumage. No matter what the weather, gamekeepers sweated their way down Gunmaker's Row in three-piece, inch-thick tweeds; the country-estate agents wore custard cords; and the CLA chaps came resplendent in Guards ties and battered panamas.

And then, of course, came the happy throng of singlet-and-tattoo aficionados, terrier on one hand, beer can in the other. The tattoos were of the basic flying swallows and 'I love mother' variety, nothing remotely as artistic as those now adorning the coccyx of the modern woman. (I asked one if she knew that the hennaed hieroglyphic meant, 'I work in the fishmongers' in Cantonese. She didn't - but then, neither did I.)

The Game Fair has never been a redoubt of political correctness but in the Eighties the whole concept would have been laughable. The World Pheasant Association, run by Keith and Jean Howman, was renowned for its saucy T-shirts sold by svelte helpers. The emblazoned mottos, such as 'Laid in aid of WPA' and 'I've Got A Splendid Pair', were never subtle - but they did generate a lot of PR and smiles.

Game Fair hotels were never far from some Wodehousian rioting, and there was an especially memorable 3am battle between rival shooting magazines armed with a savage armoury of sardine sandwiches. Direct action was also favoured by one very well-known lady who, tired of the endless parties, would slope off to the public car parks armed with a half-brick. Whenever she saw a dog locked in a car with closed windows, she happily smashed a back window and left a note under the windscreen saying: 'Your dog was about to die of heat exhaustion. I broke your window to save it. Please ring me if you wish to take this further.' She never received a phone call, let alone a complaint.

Another highlight was the World Pigeon Plucking Competition, if only because of the tense test of public-address pronouncement it caused the Game Fair secretary (legendary for his five-minute demands for some poor soul to shift his car). The air would fill with feathers and occasionally wings as everyone from nine-year-olds to balding game-dealers would try for the title.

Today, the show is more professional and commercial, but the flame of countryside independence and fun still burns strongly, and nowhere is it tended more fiercely than on The Field's *stand.*

Jonathan Young, Editor *The Field*

Another prominent field sports journalist who can be found at almost every Game Fair is Robin Scott. It was not long after Robin attended his first fair at Kinmount in 1978 that it became an occupational necessity as well as a pleasure; he was appointed Editor of *Sporting Gun* in 1986.

'The social side of the Fair is by far the most important aspect' he says. 'I look forward enormously to meeting readers and old friends at the Fair.

'The sport of shooting is now in a healthier state than it's ever been, and the Game Fair has played a very important role in this. Over the years I've been involved, we have managed to pull together in the face of opposition from several quarters. It's done our sport an enormous amount of good.'

Bernard Cribbins, one of the most familiar faces in England through his work in films and television for well over half a century, is also a lifelong angler and shooting man. He is one of the many Game Fair regulars who go principally to meet up with old friends. 'I've been visiting the Fair since the 1970s' he says. 'It's a wonderful way to relax and chat with the many wonderful people I've got to know through fishing and shooting over the years. I usually spend at least half a day on Fisherman's Row, going up and down the line to talk to people I haven't seen since the last Fair.'

Bernard, who celebrates his 80th birthday at the end of this year, still goes fishing regularly and is closely involved with the Wheelyboat Trust, whose work enables many disabled anglers to overcome access problems to fishing waters. He has just finished making a new angling series called *Catching the Impossible*, filmed by Hugh Miles, who made the enormously successful *A Passion For Angling*.

For many visitors the Game Fair is all about gundogs. Today the owner can enter a dog in an enormous variety of events, including the CLA Scurry, Scramble, Pick-up, Dog & Gun events and the BASC Bulldog and Snooker scurries. They can also watch training demonstrations from experts such as John and Sandra Halstead or Ian and Wendy Openshaw, or visit the working-dog ring to admire displays and parades by dozens of different breeds.

Large crowds are attracted to the two major gundog events of the summer months, the International Team Competition between England, Scotland, Wales and Ireland - the most exciting and crowd-pleasing event in the Game Fair calendar - and the Euro Challenge, a relatively new event but a great crowd-puller.

Clay shooting has been a part of the Fair since the very beginning, and today some 2000 people take part in the competitions or sign up for instruction. The Game Fair Championship draws hundreds of entries, while there are daily 50-bird competitions and specialist competitions such as the Celebrity top shots event, the Press shoot, Gun Trade shoot, BASC shoot and instructional shooting.

The amount of work involved in the siting, construction and operation of the clay shooting lines is immense. For the past eight years they have been the responsibility of John Bidwell, five times World FITASC Champion, twice European Champion, British Champion and holder of many other titles too numerous to mention. John is kept so busy - he puts on shooting demonstrations as well as running the clay lines - that he says he has not had time to visit the rest of the Fair since 2000.

These days more than 60 staff are employed on the lines, operating 120 traps. Siting the clay lines is always a difficult task. The layout has to be as close to the body of the Game Fair as possible, but not so close that the constant barrage of gunfire is too intrusive, or that safety becomes an issue.

Safety can be an issue for the fishing events too, where careful precautions are necessary to ensure no one is hit by a high-speed lure. Michael Evans, who has managed the casting events at the Fair since 1994, has experienced some of the more subtle hazards of running a live event a few feet away from crowds of people.

'I have a love-hate relationship with the PA system' he says. 'However hard we plan and test, the ever-present fear is that a microphone will pack up when a demonstrator is in full flow.

'One year the system worked each time it was tested - and then failed every time a demonstration began. Finally the engineer realised that the signal was being blocked by the crowds. They would flock in and the system would fail. Then they would get fed up and leave again, and it would start working.'

Michael is unlikely to forget the time a golden eagle which had escaped from a falconry display flapped nonchalantly past his rod tip, giving him the shock of his life.

There is so much to see, so much to do, that three days simply doesn't seem long enough.

Some things about the Game Fair are timeless. The scent of bruised grass as you step eagerly out of your car after a long and tedious journey. The distant rattle of musketry from the clay ground, the long slog to the tented city far off, all white canvas and fluttering flags like the army of Richard the Lionheart encamped outside Jerusalem.

We dress for the occasion, be it in panama hat and linen jacket or a vest that shows to advantage our tattoos. Keepers swelter in three-piece Harris Tweed suits on the hottest day of the year. Ferret handlers in cammo coats chat to masters of hounds, wildfowlers talk shot sizes with driven-grouse men. Falconers discuss the season past with shoot captains, while every breed of sporting dog is represented and towed round reluctantly, wishing to be elsewhere. If they are not involved in the official gundog events, one wonders what on earth they are doing there. Best not to enquire too closely.

Time was, and how we loved it, when dear old Tom Forrest, the late lamented gamekeeper from The Archers, *addressed the crowd over the Tannoy. It all added to the illusion and sense of unreality. If it was not old Tom it was the Game Fair Secretary, who spoke throatily in a wood-alcohol voice, like a crusty Brigadier after a good dinner at his club. That sound has long been replaced on the mike by the now universal Estuary English.*

Holland and Holland paraded their dray horses towing a fine equipage, which was taking customers to a clay-shooting lesson. The best anglers in the world swished their lines, the scent of frying bacon wafted with onions on its breath, thirsty fair goers 'in the know' dropped into certain stands and were invited 'round the back', for the Game Fair could be a dry old place.

Magazines wooed potential subscribers with special offers, famous sporting names appeared in the flesh, often a disappointment, for idols often are best kept at arm's length. Mostly people mingled and trudged, unable, with the best of planning and fortitude, to see more than half the Fair in one day. Feet ache and faces redden; they are burdened down by a welter of purchases, to be regretted long before they reach the car for the homeward journey.

For all its quirkiness and latter-day commercialism, the Game Fair has become an icon, something at which to be seen. Once unique, it has spawned dozens of regional imitators. They may ape many of its practices, but the Game Fair remains the big one, and it will never quite be replaced by the Nether Wallop Game and Country Fair down the road.

For fifty years it has flourished. Some years, certainly, have been better then others, but I for one have always enjoyed its rich flavour. I have not missed one since Burleigh in the mid-Sixties. Happy memories throng for attention, such as sitting on an upturned crate at the back of Shooting Times *stand talking shooting with the late Hugh Falkus and Macdonald Hastings, father of Max, who continues the family passion for the field and its sports.*

John Humphreys, *Shooting Times*

Sooner than you would have thought possible, it is Sunday afternoon and the stallholders are beginning to pack for the journey home. The cannier Fairgoers are out now in force, looking for those wonderful bargains that the final day offers to those who are patient enough not to spend all their money early on. Others, hoping to beat the inevitable queues to get back on the road, are already bumping their way towards the gates.

For the organisers, mountains of work lie ahead. They must 'demob' and restore the site, pack equipment, tidy everything away, thank everyone who must be thanked and bring the whole event to a professional conclusion. For them, the work never really stops. For the rest of us, however, the Game Fair is over. Until next year.

What of the future?

'The Game Fair is now a mature business, and like all mature businesses we must be constantly on the alert for change' says Vincent Hedley Lewis. 'We must pay great attention to the world we are operating in and continue to diversify to meet its needs.

'At the same time we must never lose sight of our core values. The Fair is still principally about promoting country sports and explaining to the wider world what goes on in the countryside.'

'A day at the Game Fair has to be fun and relaxing, and this can only be achieved through professional organisation. Its future success depends on having a professional team directing affairs. I am proud to have inherited a superb team of directors and managers whose experience and skills are exceptional.

'If we hold fast to the vision for another 50 years, the Game Fair Centenary will be something to look forward to.'

The Country Land and Business Association

The Country Land and Business Association (CLA), who are proud to organise The CLA Game Fair on behalf of everyone involved in rural life and business, is the premier membership organisation for the owners and managers of land, property and businesses in rural England and Wales. It has been looking after landowners' interests since its foundation in the days of rural depression in 1907, when the country was a much simpler place in which to live, work and trade.

Originally CLA stood for Central Land Association. The name was changed to the Central Landowners' Association and later the Country Landowners' Association before finally taking its present form.

With a membership now standing at 36,000, the Association has long been recognised by the Government as the official voice of landowners and rural business in England and Wales. Over the century since its birth, landowners have had to learn to contend with an increasingly complex array of laws as well as ever-greater pressures on the countryside from all quarters. Against this background, the CLA continues to fight the land manager's corner in local and national government as well as advising its members on a wide variety of matters including law, taxation, land use, renewables, planning, business, and the rural economy.

The organisation of The CLA Game Fair is a very important annual activity of the CLA. Members benefit from free and discounted tickets and the CLA Members' Enclosure is an important feature.

The CLA's main objectives for The CLA Game Fair are:

1. To ensure The CLA Game Fair is the annual exhibition to showcase country sports and promote them to as wide an audience as possible.

2. To offer the best possible environment/platform for rural businesses to present themselves to as great a number of visitors as possible.

CLA PAST PRESIDENTS

1957-1959 Sir John Ruggles-Brise Bt OBE TD DL

1959-1961 Lt Col R B Verdin OBE TD DL

1961-1963 R B Verney

1963-1965 The Lord De Ramsey

1965-1967 Brig A F L Clive DSO MC DL

1967-1969 N Strutt TD DL

1969-1971 G Howard

1971-1973 C Graham

1973-1975 G B Heywood

1975-1977 Sir John Quicke CBE DL

1977-1979 R H Paul OBE

1979-1981 G D Lillingston DL

1981-1983 The Lord Middleton MC DL

1983-1985 P Giffard

1985-1987 J H M Norris CBE DL

1987-1989 G E Lee-Steere DL

1989-1991 R N Swarbrick CBE DL

1991-1993 The Lord De Ramsey DL FRAgS

1993-1995 A H Duberly CBE

1995-1997 The Lord Cameron of Dillington DL FRICS

1997-1999 I D R MacNicol

1999-2001 S A Bosanquet

2001-2003 Sir Edward Greenwell Bt DL

2003-2005 M H Hudson

2005-2007 E D Fursdon

THE CLA GAME FAIR MANAGEMENT/ADVISORY BOARD

The Fair is controlled by The CLA Game Fair Board, which has gone through various names and changes over the years. The Chairmen have been:

To 1978   George Lillingstone Esq

1978 - 1984   Sam Whitbread Esq

1985 - 1991 Roger Graham-Parker Esq

1992 - 1997 James Gibson Fleming Esq

1998 - 2005 The Hon. Richard Godber

2006 - Present Vincent Hedley Lewis Esq

THE CLA GAME FAIR LOCAL COMMITTEE CHAIRMEN

Each year a voluntary Local Committee is appointed to assist the permanent staff with the organisation of the various events and features. The time so generously given by the Chairman and the many members of the Local Committee, along with an enormous number of stewards, is at the heart of The Game Fair's success.

1958 The Rt Hon The Earl of Ellesmere

1959 The Right Hon The Viscount Camrose

1960 George Howard Esq

1961 Brigadier A L Matthews

1962 Lt Col S A F Egerton

1963 Col N V Stopford Sackville CBE

1964 Major General F C C Graham CB DSO

1965 Col Peter Fleming OBE

1966 Lt Col W H Olivier TD DL JP

1967 Major E R W Robinson MC

1968 Major General F C C Graham CB DSO

1969 Col P H Lloyd CBE TD DL JP

1970 Lt Col J L B Leicester-Warren TD VL JP

1971 Roger Parker-Jarvis Esq

1972 R H Pardoe TD FRICS

1973 Major General F C C Graham CB DSO

1974 Brig Sir Richard A-G-Calthorpe CBE LLD JP

1975 Lt Col W H Olivier TD DL JP

1976 C R Woosnam Esq

1977 J F Robinson TD DL JP

1978 A M Bell Macdonald

1979 G J Ward

1980 Col T E Forman Hardy CBE MC TD DL

1981 The Hon R Godber

1982 R C Roundell

1983 Col R C Stewart CBE

1984 Commander C J Balfour RN

1985 Lord Guernsey

1986 Col E C York

1987 Lt Col J R G Stanton MBE

1988 Major F M Strang Steel

1989 C A J Oliver-Bellasis Esq FRICS

1990 F E S Hayes Esq

1991 Sir William Morton CBL DL

1992 M A T Trevor-Barnston Esq

1993 W A Balfour Esq

1994 The Hon Maurice Robson

1995 J D M Stoddart-Scott Esq

1996 Sir Henry Nevile KCVO

1997 Cdr Michael Saunders Watson CBE DL

1998 Sir James Scott Bt

1999 T J P Hare Esq

2000 T Loyd Esq

2001 V R Hedley Lewis Esq

2002 M P Maclay esq

2003 F S Boddy Esq

2004 Mrs C Aston

2005 C H C Coaker Esq

2006 M P Lowry Esq

2007 C W Bourne-Arton Esq

2008 H St John Esq

Among the many unpaid servants of The Game Fair are the members of the Management Board. They offer advice on a wide range of skills, from event management, retailing and financial matters to the countryside and the sporting and leisure industries. Sam Whitbread, Frank McBratney and David Griffiths have served for many years on the Board, freely giving their advice and time.

The Game Fair Management Board at the 50th Anniversary are:

Vincent Hedley Lewis Esq - Chairman
William Worsley Esq
John Taylor Esq
Frank McBratney Esq
Sir James Scott
Tony Worth Esq
Richard Ferrand Esq
Martin Brocklehurst
Charles Benson
Adrian Gane Esq
Chris Murray

The Permanent Team at the 50th Anniversary are:

Show Director - David Hough
Director of Marketing and Show Development - Fiona Eastman
Head of Sponsorship - Nicky Barr
Head of Site Management - Nick Brookes Ward
Accountant - Jane Pyle
Exhibitor Manager - Stephen Ingram
Traffic Management - Tony Wall
Press Officer - Marishelle Gibson
Exhibitor Assistant - Chesca Oszczyk
Office Administrator - Tracy-Leigh Reed
Sponsorship Assistant - Diane Powell
PR Assistant - Karen Bartleet

Assisting in the on-site Organiser's Office:
Lady Sarah Luke
Sally Wetherall
Caroline Labouchere